God's Partners

Lay Christians at Work

Lay Christians at Work

God's Partners

STANLEY J. MENKING
BARBARA WENDLAND

Judson Press ® Valley Forge

God's Partners

Bible quotations in this volume are from the following translations: New Revised Standard Version of the Bible, copyrighted 1989 by the Division of Christian Education of the National Council of the Churches of Christ in the United States of America, and are used by permission. All rights reserved. The Revised Standard Version of the Bible, copyrighted 1946, 1952, 1971, 1973, by the Division of Christian Education of the National Council of the Churches of Christ in the U.S.A., and used by permission. All rights reserved. HOLY BIBLE New International Version, copyright 1978, New York International Bible Society. Used by permission. *The New English Bible,* Copyright The Delegates of the Oxford University Press and The Syndics of the Cambridge University Press 1961, 1970. The *Good News Bible,* the Bible in Today's English Version. Copyright American Bible Society, 1976. Used by permission.

Library of Congress Cataloging-in-Publication Data
Menking, Stanley J. 1932–
    God's partners: lay Christians at work/by Stanley J. Menking and Barbara Wendland.
    p. cm.
    Includes bibliographical references.
    ISBN 0-8170-1196-X
    1. Lay ministry. 2. Laity. I. Wendland, Barbara. II. Title.
BV677.M46 1993   93-30829

Printed in the U.S.A.

Table of Contents

Introduction
An Invitation from Barbara

In this book Stan Menking and I discuss what we see God calling men and women to be and do in their workplaces, homes, and churches, and we offer some ideas about how we think the church can carry out its God-given mission more effectively. We invite you to join our conversation by adding your thoughts and feelings to ours as you read.

Stan is a clergyman and a seminary professor, and I'm a laywoman whose main contact with the church has been as a volunteer in a local congregation. Both of us are concerned about the church and especially about the role of the laity in it. Even though we agree on many things, because of our different experiences we see the issues somewhat differently and sometimes come to different conclusions.

In our book Stan presents the theological basis for the ministry of the laity, while I raise the kinds of questions that lay women and men often have. We hope our conversation will help you raise your own questions and find satisfying answers, so that you can do more of what God is calling you to do and help the church become more nearly what God wants it to be.

I didn't choose the church

When I started going to church, it wasn't by choice. My parents had me baptized as a baby, and at the prescribed time I "joined the church" along with everyone else in my fourth-grade Sunday school class. I didn't join because of any personal conviction. I joined only because I knew it was what I was supposed to do.

What I remember about joining the church isn't anything spiritual or even pleasant. I remember what happened to my dress. While I was waiting for Mama to be ready I stood by her dresser, talking to her and playing with her lipstick while she combed her hair and put on her makeup. I dropped the open lipstick on the new pale-pink dress I was wearing, leaving an ugly red streak that Mama's frantic efforts with cleaning fluid couldn't completely remove. It was not a happy morning.

Throughout my growing-up years I went to church regularly with my parents, and when I married, my pattern of church participation continued unchanged. I thought of going to church in the same way I thought of making my bed or brushing my teeth: I knew I was supposed to do it, so I did it. What I thought and felt about it didn't seem to matter, so I kept quiet.

For about forty years I reacted this way to everything the authorities in my life seemed to expect of me. When questions, doubts, or negative feelings arose, I banished them from my mind as quickly as possible. All the people I respected told me that was the only right way to live, and I believed them.

At midlife, after all those years of unquestioning conformity, I suddenly realized that some of the nonconforming thoughts and feelings I thought I had banished forever were still around. In fact, some of them were rising up and clamoring for attention. Finally, I couldn't ignore them any longer.

Surprising changes

About the same time, my lifelong habit of reading blossomed mysteriously into what seemed like an intensive, custom-designed course of study, as if I were being prepared for a specific job. I kept feeling drawn from one book or topic to another in a strange but logical sequence, even though I had barely been aware of some of them before.

In order to make contact with other people who were reading and thinking about the same things I was, I went to graduate school at a seminary, although most of my earlier impressions of seminaries had been negative. As time went on I often found myself agreeing with people I had formerly criticized and learning exciting new things that I hadn't realized I wanted to know. Soon I started speaking to new audiences and writing for publication for the first time in my life. I kept finding myself involved in all sorts of interesting new projects that would have been unthinkable for me in earlier years.

I slowly realized that the acceptance of a belief or custom by admirable people over a long period of time didn't necessarily make that belief true or that custom desirable. Nor did the fact that a person was older than I or in a position of greater authority or prominence mean that that person's ideas were right and mine were wrong. And I saw that opinions weren't necessarily right just because they were held by the majority. Most important of all, I saw that God was behind the changes I was experiencing. I realized that God was prodding me to question familiar patterns and to venture out in new directions.

Questions about the church

Taking a fresh look at the church has been an important part of this process. I've seen that many traditional religious practices are of human origin and can be changed without going against God's wishes. In fact, I've become convinced that some of our traditional practices urgently need changing because they go against God's wishes.

In a sense the whole Bible is the story of God's efforts to reveal more about God. These efforts have often involved wrenching people loose from strongly held beliefs and cherished traditional practices that don't conform to God's will. Ironically, the most religious people have often put up the strongest resistance to God's efforts. I think God is still trying to show us more of God and trying to get us to change religious and social customs that hinder God's purposes, yet we church members are the ones resisting those efforts now.

Some of our customs probably arose because people misunderstood God's intentions. Others were needed at an earlier stage in human history but are no longer appropriate. Like habits and rules that are important for toddlers but unsuitable for older children or adults, some of our religious traditions may not fit our present situation. Other customs may have begun as valid responses to God's instructions, but they have become distorted over time as people changed them to suit their own wishes. God keeps working to show us where we've gone astray, but we often refuse to act on the new insights God offers us.

In recent years I've become concerned about helping the church recognize God's nudges and act on them. I want the church to turn loose of some outmoded, ineffective, and even harmful ways of functioning and get busy with the ministries to which God is calling it in today's world.

Unfortunately, many church members today seem unaware that God is calling them to do anything. Some have given up on the church and dropped out. Others have stayed only as names on church rolls, or as bodies in pews on widely scattered Sundays when they happen not to have anything they'd rather do. I'd like to help these discouraged Christians see that there's a lot more to God than what they've found in churches so far. There's always more to God than what we've found. I want to help the church do a better job of communicating with people, meeting their real needs, and enabling them to minister to the world's needs.

When I examine my understanding of the church's mission and the ways the church goes about carrying out that mission, I come up with a lot of questions. Instead of trying to banish them from my mind as I once did, I'm asking them openly now. For example, I question the sharp distinction that we make between laity and clergy. It doesn't seem to fit the kind of church the Bible describes, and it didn't exist in the earliest years of the church. I'm sure that God intends every Christian to minister to others, that God wants ministry to be largely a do-it-yourself job for each of us, not just a job that we hire professionals to do for us. I'm also sure that God intends Christians to minister to the world at large, not just to each other. Our failure to follow God's will in this regard has caused both laity and clergy to suffer.

Over the centuries we've strayed from God's will in other ways, too. We've come to see the church mainly as the passive guardian of sacred statements about God, expressed in the language of ancient times and remote cultures. I believe God wants the church to communicate in ways that today's people will hear and understand, rather than simply preserving the words and practices of the distant past. I think God wants the church to be not a museum but a living, up-to-the-minute demonstration of what God has in mind for today's world.

Besides being concerned about the church as a body, I'm also concerned about its members as individuals, particularly those who are women. In many ways our society treats women as if their abilities and interests were completely unimportant. This goes against what Christians claim to believe about the use of talents and gifts.

Our pattern of male leadership in the church seems to have been established by human beings and not by God, so I don't see anything sinful about changing it. I suspect that what's sinful is refusing to change it, but unfortunately the church often refuses. I'm confident that the current reevaluation of men's and women's traditional roles is being led by God, not just by women, and I want to help the church promote the changes God is asking us to make.

I've chosen the church now

As a child I had no choice about being part of the church, but as a middle-aged woman I chose to remain part of it. I intend to stick with it from now on, because I'm convinced that despite its short-comings the church is the world's only real hope. The church has a vital God-given mission: to show the world what God is like and to bring people to Christ through ministries of love, justice, and healing. Without taking an honest look at the church and at ourselves and then making the changes that we see are needed, we can't carry out our mission effectively. These changes will be painful, of course, and will include making some mistakes, but failure to change may well be fatal.

My contributions to this book are part of my effort to look honestly at the church and at the changes that I believe God is calling us to make. I invite you to join me. Start by considering some questions about what I've said, then meet Stan.

Questions for Reflection

Take time right now to think about your responses to these questions if you are reading this book by yourself, or to talk about them if you are using it in a group. Do this with the questions that follow each section. As you read the book, especially if you are doing it by yourself, you may also find writing your answers to the questions helpful. We recommend using a private notebook that you can use regularly for your reflections about what God is calling you to do. A looseleaf notebook works well, because it lets you insert later insights when they occur to you.

1. If you are a church member, what do you remember about your entry into the church? If you grew up participating in a church regularly, how did you feel about it?

2. How have your feelings and church participation changed as you have grown older?

3. Have you ever been aware that God was trying to nudge you into new directions? How have you responded? How will you respond to the nudges you are aware of now?

4. What do you see as the purpose of the church? How does this compare to your experience or observation of what churches do?

5. How does your view of women's role in society, and of the church's influence on it, compare with Barbara's?

6. What other feelings or thoughts came to you as you read this part of the introduction?

An Invitation from Stan

I invite you to join Barbara and me as we examine our understanding of what God calls lay men and women to do and be. We'll discuss some points that our experience has led us to think are especially important, and as you read what we say you'll undoubtedly come up with other important points to consider.

You'll see that Barbara and I don't always agree with each other. There probably will be times when you don't agree with either of us, and that's fine. We both think that asking questions and considering different viewpoints are important for clarifying what you believe and for making the changes that are a necessary part of growing in faith.

Thinking about faith

Theology is my profession, which means that my main occupation is thinking about the Christian faith on behalf of the church. I believe that a theologian's job is to explore the issues that arise out of the church's life and mission, and for many years I've had an intense interest in doing some of that exploration. But theology is not for professionals alone.

Many centuries ago a leader of the Christian church said that theology was faith seeking understanding. This means that when you think about your faith, trying to understand what you believe and why you believe it, you are a theologian even if theology is not your main occupation. The main thing God calls you to do as a layperson is to minister to others in the everyday world where you live and work, but in order to do this most effectively you need to think about your faith. You have to be at least a part-time theologian, and I hope this book will help you do that.

For over thirty years the ministry of the laity has been the main aspect of theology that has occupied my attention. My interest began when I began serving as a pastor in my last year of college. I was a local-church pastor for thirteen years, through my theological studies in seminary and the additional time I spent getting a doctoral degree. During these years I had to minister to the needs of the laity, but laypeople also ministered to me while I studied theology. The needs of these women and men undoubtedly gave me one reason for looking at the issue of lay ministry.

During my student years the church recovered its awareness of the importance of lay ministry. This renewed awareness arose from a new appreciation of the church as the people of God. Hendrik Kramer's pioneer study *The Theology of the Laity* and Yves Congar's book *The People of God* became classics and interested me in looking at the issue of lay ministry.

Like many other theologians at that time, I was also inspired by the work of the lay academies that arose in Germany after World War II and found a way to reflect seriously on the unique needs of German laypeople. Later the ministry of the laity also attracted significant attention from Vatican II, helping me to see that if the church was indeed the people of God, the ministry of the laity was an integral part of the church's ministry.

During these years there was also a deep concern about the issue of justice in the world. The work of the German martyr Dietrich Bonhoeffer and the insights found in his *Letters and Papers from Prison* caused many people to attribute a new importance to the world as the place where laypeople carried out their ministry.

At the same time theologians became concerned about the issue of secularization. In contrast to secularism — conforming to the world's ways with no reference to God — secularization was the process by which the gospel made humankind responsible to God for the care of creation. Secularization was the product of the gospel, and the secular world was the domain of the laity. Encountering these theological issues added to my interest in exploring the ministry of the laity.

Upon completing my graduate studies I joined the staff of a large suburban church. My job was to relate its congregation to the needs of a nearby urban community in an effort to express the ministry of the laity in a "worldly" context. This unusual assignment gave me the opportunity to work both theologically and practically with laypeople in ministry. I saw the need to ask what our beliefs meant for the ministry of the laity and what contributions the study of theology needed to make in order to support this ministry.

In 1977 my job responsibilities changed to the area of theological education. Since then, one of my main responsibilities has been to work with pastors who are working toward the Doctor of Ministry degree. These pastors serve full-time in churches while working on the degree, and as part of their degree requirements they must develop ministry projects that involve working with the laity. My work with this degree program has therefore included advising clergy about issues related to the ministry of the laity.

Ministry in the church

The ministry of the laity is not a new feature of the church. The early church was a lay movement whose growth may have been due as much to migrating Christians – lay men and women – as to the apostle Paul. Jesus himself was a layman, and his inner circle of disciples were laypeople. Clergy rose to prominence in the church only as the church began to grow. The church came to need standards of belief (creeds), approved sources of faith (the Bible), and a way of identifying the legitimate exercise of authority (apostolic succession), and this led to professional leadership. In this process laypeople were gradually changed from doers of ministry to supporters and receivers of ministry.

Occasionally in the Middle Ages this pattern was challenged, sometimes by laypeople who were heads of states (Constantine and Charlemagne) and at other times by those whose personal piety went against the established patterns (St. Francis and Peter Waldo). These challenges, however, did not bring about any real change in the normal forms of ministry.

The Reformation brought another short-lived challenge. Protestantism aimed at ending the clergy's special status as the only doers of ministry, but Protestant practice has not lived up to its promise. This failure is evident in the reluctance of many Protestant denominations to give the laity equal representation with the clergy in setting the denominations' policies. Even in denominations that now theoretically give the laity an equal voice, laypeople come and go in church-government bodies, while those who are ordained retain membership in these bodies for their entire careers, giving them greater power. Churches have tried to limit clerical power in some ways, such as requiring pastors to change congregations periodically, but even these policies haven't changed the basic power relationship of clergy and laity.

In making these observations I don't want to portray the clergy exclusively as the villains or the laity as the victims. Both lay and ordained people get caught up in the normal patterns that characterize all movements as they age. In any institution, benefits that come from being a part of the institution make its members want to keep things the way they are.

For clergy, the ordained ministry is a job as well as a call from God. Clergy see their job as being leaders of their congregations, and leaders must have followers. Clergy also see their job as ministering to the people in their congregations. So laypeople are the people that clergy expect to lead and minister to. Consequently, clergy try to lead the laity into an understanding of ministry that meets their own need to succeed as leaders and ministers.

In addition, someone has to take care of the church as an institution and officially represent it in the eyes of the world. Lay women and men, busy with the responsibilities of their daily lives, usually leave these jobs to the clergy. Also, laypeople need caring ministry themselves, and they want it done by someone who is trained and available. The practical solution has been to let clergy fill this role. This system has continued because both the laity and clergy have felt that its benefits outweighed its costs.

Sometimes we assume that if laypeople would take charge of the church, it would be reborn. Most people, however, tend to assume that the Christian faith affirms their cultural norms, so they rarely see any need to change these patterns. It seems unlikely, then, to expect that if the laity were in charge and could rule the church by majority vote the church would become more faithful to God's will for it.

The church's mandate is not determined by majority votes. In fact, the twenty centuries of Christian history show that the most faithful ministries are usually advocated and carried out by a minority. So the question is not who will control the church's life. Rather, the question is how the church will support the part of its ministry that can only be done by laypeople. This understanding of the question gives both the clergy and laity a new agenda.

A theology of lay ministry

Unfortunately the ministry of the laity is often evaluated only in terms of what it contributes to the gathered life of the community of faith. Church leaders worry about how to get more laypeople involved in church activities. The tragic irony of this view is that Christians who participate in forms of service that are not "church-centered" assume that they are not engaged in ministry. They think that ministry is only what is done in and for the church. This view presents the most serious and formidable obstacle to letting a true theology of lay ministry shape the life of a congregation.

Taken seriously, a theology of the ministry of the laity is a radical challenge to the life of the church. Like other contemporary liberation theologies, it can create surprising alliances that will overcome old conflicts because it strikes at the very root of the church's practices.

Theologies of lay ministry, however, occupy only a small part of the total volume of current theological discussion, and most of them, unfortunately, are second-hand, relying on the clergy for expression. This lessens the credibility of a theology of lay ministry for those it tries to support and also for those it challenges.

Writing this book is an effort to involve more laypeople in thinking about their faith as a whole and about the role of the laity in the church in particular. When it comes to a theology of lay ministry, laypeople are the theologians the church most needs to hear from. I hope that reading this book will help you to think about your faith and then to express your thoughts. The church needs to hear them.

In this book I hope first to identify the main theological issues that are important for the ministry of the laity and then to offer a way of thinking about those issues that will encourage and support laypeople in doing their ministries. Lay men and women need to realize that the theological issues that they encounter in their day-to-day work are profound. And the church needs to see that these issues require serious theological reflection, for they go to the very heart of the gospel.

Most of all, I want to affirm the laypeople who are engaged in ministry, the pastors who are responsible for supporting them, and all Christians who reflect theologically on the ministry of the laity. What they are doing is vitally important.

In this book we will look at the ministry of the laity by exploring the belief that all human beings are created in God's image. Our study will include examining six major theological categories in which the ministry of the laity is prominent:

1. Who are human beings in relation to God's purpose for the world?
2. What does the world of work in which laypeople live look like?
3. What is the role of Jesus Christ?
4. What are the gifts of the Holy Spirit?
5. What is the church's role as a sign of the image of God within each of us?

6. How does the concept of the kingdom of God represent the fulfillment of what was begun at creation, consummating the labors of the laity?

Let's get started.

Questions for Reflection

1. When Stan was beginning his work as a pastor he found that laypeople ministered to him when he had expected to be ministering to them instead. What experiences can you remember of being helped by someone you were expecting to help?

2. What experiences, people, or books contributed to your choice of your life work or life patterns?

3. What was your first job experience as an adult? How has your work changed since then?

4. To what extent do you think laity should be doers of the church's ministry, and to what extent should they be supporters and receivers of it?

5. If you are active in a church, do you think the relationship between the clergy and laity needs to be changed? If so, how might this be accomplished? How could you help to bring it about?

6. We have stated that "the church's mandate is not determined by majority votes" and that "opinions [aren't] necessarily right just because they [are] held by the majority." Do you agree? How much weight should the church give to the views of the majority? If not the majority of its members, who should decide what policies the church will follow?

7. Why are most theologies of lay ministry expressed by clergy instead of laypeople? Lack of interest? Lack of opportunity to get involved in the church's theological conversations? Lack of time or training? How could laypeople play a more prominent part in expressing the church's theology?

8. What other thoughts or feelings came to you as you read Stan's part of the introduction?

Chapter 1

Who Am I?

Stan: You May Be More Than You Think You Are

The alarm goes off. Monday morning. Time to think about facing it all again. You were busy at church yesterday, but what's the use of that now, you wonder. Does what you hear at church really matter when it comes to real life in the places where you live it? You ask yourself, "What would happen if I really acted the way we talk about in church? Do I dare?" You think about trying a little of it, and sometimes you do it, but a lot of the time your good intentions fall by the wayside. Well, there's no time to worry about such things right now. Time to get up.

You may think you're the only person who ever asks these questions, so you hesitate to ask them out loud. That would let those churchy people know that your faith is weak. How embarrassing that would be! You wouldn't want to risk it. Besides, you have a hunch that the answers they would give wouldn't help. People who act so religious don't seem to have any idea of what you have to cope with every day. They must not know what the real world is like.

Still, you can't help thinking about what the Bible says, and about what God expects of you. Sometimes you wonder, "Am I being the person God wants me to be? Am I doing what God wants me to do?" But who could ask anyone questions like these without feeling like a real oddball? It's safer to keep quiet.

In any case, if you asked your friends they'd probably just tell you what you already know—that you're taking care of yourself and your family, you're doing a good job at work, you're a good citizen (most of the time, at least), and you like to have a good time too, and there's certainly nothing wrong with that. "Don't worry about all that other stuff!" your friends would conclude.

That doesn't really help, does it? It doesn't address your deepest questions: "Does what I do really matter? Am I important in the whole scheme of things? Am I valued only for what I know, what I can do, and what I have? Does anybody value me just for being me? If so, who am I?"

You are God's partner

Biblical faith says you are God's partner. To God you aren't a slave whose only duty is to do what you are told. You aren't even an employee who agrees to do work in exchange for pay. You are a real partner whom God invites to share the responsibility for carrying out God's plan for the world.

This means that the real world you live in every day is not God-forsaken. God cares about everyone, every place, and every time — every detail. Everything about your life matters to God. Nothing is too little to be important.

What's more, nothing is too big for God to share with you. That's hard to believe! If it's true, it presents you with a challenge that feels overwhelming. But no matter how unbelievable it may seem, or how overwhelmed you may feel, God keeps inviting you to partnership.

This is God's answer to your deepest longings. God made this offer to you at the beginning of time and keeps offering it to you daily. When you ask, "Who am I?" God answers, "My partner."

One way in which the Bible describes this partnership is by saying that human beings are created in God's image. Partnership with God is for everyone. It is not reserved for special people, not even clergy or missionaries or anyone else who works full-time on church activities. As a layperson you are a full partner with God. Your whole life, not just what you do in the church or on its behalf, is your contribution to the partnership.

That sounds good, doesn't it? But when you watch the TV news or read the morning paper it's hard to believe that God is in charge and that the world is full of God's partners. The partnership doesn't seem to have much effect on daily life. Critics of the Christian faith try to use this as evidence to show that Christians are deluding themselves when they claim that God is in charge and that human beings are God's partners, created in God's image. You can probably find plenty of evidence to refute such criticism. You know of people who do selfless work for the good of humanity. The world is not a total wasteland. Still, sometimes it's hard to be sure that the critics are wrong.

The main evidence that seems to support them is closer to home: you know what your own thoughts and feelings are like, and how often you fail to do what you probably should do. Your own behavior doesn't always furnish much evidence that you are God's partner. How can you believe that you really are in partnership with God? What does it mean to be in partnership with God?

These are the same questions that were asked by the people who first heard the creation stories that are included in the Bible, in the book of Genesis (chapters 1 and 2). The story of Adam and Eve says that God created us. It also says that we were created to care for the rest of God's world.

We see this when God gives Adam and Eve the task of naming the other creatures (Genesis 2:19-20). In the Hebrew tradition, on which the Old Testament is based, the power to name is more than merely the chance to put a label on something. It is the power to say what something is and what it means. It is a God-like power. This story, then, is the Bible's way of saying that God has made us co-creators, partners in creation.

God also gives Adam and Eve the job of caring for creation. This means that the world's future is in the hands of humankind, not because we have seized control of it but because God has called us to take responsibility for it. So this creation story is mainly about who we are, and about where our responsibility lies. Our responsibility—our calling—comes from God's having chosen us as partners.

The Bible is realistic, and the creation story is no exception. It shows what real people are like. Adam and Eve fail to accept the responsibility that God gives them. This is one place where you can certainly see that what you read in the Bible agrees with what you observe about real life today. This leads you to wonder, "What good is it to know what God intends, when we also know that no one has ever been able to do it?"

The main point of the creation story is that it calls attention to something important about your identity: what matters most is not what you do, but who you are. What you do is a result of who you are. Jesus affirmed this when he said that a good tree will bring forth good fruit and a bad tree bad fruit (Luke 6:43-44). When the biblical creation story says that you are God's partner, it is asking you to acknowledge who you are. Only when you know who you are will you know what you are to do.

The story of Jesus is a new creation story. He shows us "in person" what it means to be a partner with God. That is why the Christian faith says there was something special about Jesus. Jesus lets you know that simply being human doesn't keep anyone from being God's partner, because Jesus was fully human as well as fully God. Jesus shows you who you are and invites you to accept your true identity. He shows you that you are human but that you are also God-like in some ways. Jesus asks you, "Will you believe that you are God's partner?"

The next question is whether you actually live as God's partner, but this question has meaning only after you have come to terms with God's promise of partnership. Jesus Christ makes clear that to be created in God's image means being a partner. So the message in the Old Testament story of creation and the story of Jesus the Christ is the same: to know that you are God's partner is to know who you are.

Being God's partner makes a difference

Being God's partner makes a real difference. Here are five things that happen when you live as God's partner.

First, you trust your call from God. Accept your call as good news! It may not make every decision easier, but in every situation you will know who you are intended to be, and that can give you a valuable new perspective on your decisions. As God's partner, no task is too trivial. No obstacle is insurmountable. Also, you know that you don't work alone, for God who called you is with you. You have a new and clearer picture of yourself.

The second mark of life lived in partnership with God is love. As God's partner, you are a lover of other human beings. You are to love them the way God does, and Jesus has shown us what that means.

John Calvin, a layman who led the church in Geneva during the Reformation, told his followers "not to consider men's evil intention but to look upon the image of God in them."[1] He was telling them to see other people as God sees them, because they are cre-

---

1. John Calvin, *Institutes* (Philadelphia: Westminster Press, 1960), vol. 3, book vii, sec. 6.

ated in God's image. God intends for those other people to be partners too, and you love them because you know that.

Third, living as God's partner means living on the basis of a
different vision of the future. It means standing with God and looking at the future the way God does, a future in which everyone has
a place.

Critics may dismiss this viewpoint as mere wishful thinking, but
as God's partner you know that it is the only viewpoint that has any
future. Settling for less would mean living for what will not last. So
in your everyday life you see no viable choice except to look at
people from God's viewpoint and live for God's future.

The fourth distinctive mark of partnership with God is being a
doer. You need to think about what to do, of course, but you can't
just keep thinking and never act. You must decide and then do
something. You can see Jesus functioning this way when he explains his work: "It is the Father who dwells in me doing his own
work. Believe me when I say that I am in the Father and the Father
in me; or else accept the evidence of the deeds themselves" (John
14:11, NEB). What is that work? To act to create the future that God
promises.

So you are not merely to be busy. You must be busy with the
right things. This means acting as God's partner wherever you are
and whenever you have the chance, in order to help make God's
future possible.

Finally, as God's partner who looks at things from God's viewpoint, you can see more than just what people and situations look
like on the surface. God's partners discern not only what is visible
in God's creation but also what is hidden. They see not only what is
tangible but also what is intangible. The world of the spirit, of feelings, of relationships, and of values is as real as what you can
touch, see, taste, smell, and hear. Often it is even more important.

Jan Lochman, an Eastern European theologian, reminds us,
"Creation consists not only of visible things but also of invisible
things."[2] God's partners don't have to choose between the material
world and the spiritual, because both are God's creation. To neglect either one would be to neglect your responsibility as God's
partner.

---

2. Jan Lochman, The Faith We Confess (Philadelphia: Fortress Press, 1984),
65.

New jobs and new ways of doing old ones

Living in partnership with God may mean you will have new opportunities. You may realize that God is calling you to take on new jobs, or go in new directions that you never thought about before. On the other hand, it may mean doing your present jobs in new ways. Whatever God calls you to do, the particular assignment is not what matters most. What is most important is your response to God's invitation to partnership, to live as who you really are.

Does this whole idea of being God's partner sound arrogant? You may feel uneasy about it, thinking it sounds like putting yourself on the same level with God. Being a partner, however, doesn't have to mean being an equal, and being God's partner certainly can't mean being God's equal.

Human partnerships are of many different kinds. Some people are silent partners, furnishing financial support for an undertaking but not taking part in the management of it. Some partnerships are limited partnerships, in which some partners risk less than others. In every partnership, however, all partners share some of the risks and some of the rewards.

The amazing thing about our partnership with God is that God makes us real partners. Karl Barth, one of this century's leading Christian thinkers, has put it like this: "[God] willed the existence of . . . a real partner; . . . a partner who is capable of entering into covenant-relationship with Himself."[3] Being God's partner means that you no longer stand alone in your daily life. You live in community with God as God shares with you the work of creating and shaping the world's future, and that's an important job!

Being God's partner also means that "rugged individualism" can't be your style, because God is community. This is what Christians mean by speaking of God as Trinity, "one being, in three persons"—unity in diversity. You experience God calling you to be a partner through the work of these three persons, who represent three different aspects of God's nature. They have traditionally been called Father, Son, and Holy Spirit.

This unexplainable mystery lets you know that community is

---

3. Karl Barth, *Church Dogmatics* (Edinburgh: T. & T. Clark, 1958), 3:1, 184-185.

the basic nature of God and therefore of life. This means that unity in the human community, since human beings are made in God's image, requires not conformity but diversity. For those who are made in God's image, isolation can't be the main feature of life; community is the pattern in which God's partners must live.

God creates community

In addition to showing God's invitation to partnership, the creation stories in Genesis show the community-creating aspect of God's nature. In one story God realizes it isn't good for Adam to be alone, and creates Eve. Adam could not live alone and be truly what God intended. In the other creation story in Genesis, God creates humans as male and female, and not just for the purpose of procreation, for no one can be complete alone. Only in community can a person find fulfillment.

The creation stories also let God's creatures know that they must live in community with nature. God's act of creating Adam from clay and God's instruction to Adam and Eve to care for the world portray human beings' relationship with nature. Being a partner with God means being a partner not only with other people but also with the rest of the natural world.

Another valuable insight of Jan Lochman is that God is "not a 'world-forsaking' but a 'world-seeking' God."[4] God has chosen not to be self-sufficient. Instead, God takes the initiative to reach out to human beings. That is one meaning of the biblical statement "God is love." As God's partner, then, you are called to reach out to others. Anything less would deny your partnership, for God wants all people to be partners.

You can't keep partnership to yourself. When you try, you lose your life by trying to save it. In God's loving plan for the world, there can be no "haves" and "have nots." God chooses to love all because that is who God is. God's partners are called to be and do the same.

Christians sometimes forget this. We try to separate life into the "sacred" and the "secular," and it's hard to avoid seeing things in these terms, because even though we know that God is concerned about every aspect of God's creation, we see that everything in life

---

4. Lochman, *The Faith We Confess*, 62.

does not reflect God's wishes. We try to obey God by separating things into categories and classifying one as God-like and the other un-God-like. We assume that singing in the church choir, maybe, or teaching Sunday school, or going on a spiritual retreat serves God more than attending a business meeting, handling a customer complaint, or doing routine chores. What's the difference? Only that in doing the first category of things we may be more likely to focus consciously on doing what we think God expects us to do.

Even on the days when you feel pretty good about what you are doing, you may still feel that in order to be God's partner you would have to do something different—something that you would do intentionally for the purpose of serving God. Paul Tillich, an insightful twentieth-century thinker, wrote about this dilemma. He said, "Sin is a state of things in which the holy and the secular are separated, struggling with each other and trying to conquer each other."[5] Your uneasiness is a sign of that struggle in your life.

Fortunately, what God's partners do in their daily lives is not trivial to God, and God wants you to know that, rather than to be constantly uneasy about not doing something else. God's goal is not to banish the secular and replace it with the sacred. Instead, God wants you to realize that the secular is sacred. The ground on which you stand every day in God's world is holy ground.

This means that everything you do to serve others and meet their needs, in your home, your workplace, and your community, is holy. When you "rejoice with those who rejoice and weep with those who weep" (Romans 12:15, RSV), you are creating the community that God intends. When you care for the world, try to find ways to solve problems, bring joy into people's lives, take pride in doing your work well, or do something to help someone else have a better future, you are creating community and thus being God's partner. What all these kinds of actions have in common is your willingness to be part of a larger community and to contribute to it. Your world, then, is always God's world! The Bible calls it God's kingdom.

5. Paul Tillich, *Systematic Theology* (Chicago: The University of Chicago Press, 1951), 1:218.

The hard part of partnership

I'd love to be able to tell you, "Once you accept your role as God's partner, the tough part is over." Unfortunately that's not true. In fact, once you recognize and accept your partnership with God you will have to contend with a subtle temptation. You'll be tempted to forget that you are only a partner and not God. Ironically, the hardest time to realize you are doing this is when you are consciously trying to do God's will. The surer you are that you are doing God's will, the easier it is to confuse your will with God's. So feeling sure about what you are doing doesn't mean that you are actually doing God's will.

Feeling unsure is more likely to be a good sign. Strange as it may seem, your uneasiness is a sign of hope. Your uncertainty is often God's way of reminding you that you are not entitled to make the final decisions about what you do as a partner. Great harm has been done by people who were totally sure that they were doing God's will; God's true partners are humble, not arrogant, and they keep reexamining their understanding of what God wants them to be doing.

You may also get discouraged because you recognize that you keep seeking your identity from other sources, not just from your partnership with God. But this feeling, like your uncertainty, can also be a basis for hope. Emil Brunner gives good advice on this subject when he says, "Even as a sinner man can only be understood in the light of the original Image of God, namely, as one who is living in opposition to it."[6]

So even your discontent is a sign of God's promise of partnership. As Augustine of Hippo observed many centuries ago, our hearts are restless until we find our rest in God. Your restlessness shows that you are struggling with the real issue: God's call for you to be God's partner.

Reinhold Niebuhr, a leading contemporary American Christian thinker, describes the source of our restlessness this way: "The real situation is that man who is made in the image of God is unable, precisely because of those qualities in him which are designated as

---

6. Emil Brunner, *Man in Revolt* (Philadelphia: Westminster Press, 1957), 105.

'image of God,' to be satisfied with a god who is made in man's image."[7]

The fact that your spiritual struggle continues doesn't mean that you are unable to realize what it means to be God's partner. The account of God's rest on the Sabbath in one of the Genesis creation stories lets you know that God's promise for creation will be fulfilled, and that the promise holds good for you. Your work is not something that you keep doing without any hope of reaching a goal, like being on a treadmill or climbing a hill and then seeing more hills ahead. Your work does not end, but it fulfills its purpose; it creates community. Your struggle is not in vain.

Hans Küng, a contemporary Roman Catholic theologian, says that God's promise for creation gives you "a meaning despite all meaninglessness."[8] You can be hopeful about the future in spite of your doubts and fears. Even your failure to live fully as God's partner will not cancel God's promise to you. The love that led God to create you for partnership can't be set aside by anything that you do or fail to do. That's really good news!

Jesus, God's supreme partner, shows you what God is trying to give you. Jesus opens the way for fulfilling the promise that God gave at the time of creation: God promises that the world will be transformed. Acting like God's partner in your everyday life doesn't guarantee that everything you do will succeed, but it does mean that your work in the world will not be lost. The risen Christ, not the fallen Adam, is your destiny. Life, not death, is your future.

One of God's partners

Recently I saw the story of one of God's partners shown on television. It was the second of two documentaries about Jane Elliott, a third-grade school teacher in Iowa. Twenty years ago the first of the two documentaries had shown an experiment that she did with her class soon after Martin Luther King's tragic death.

Jane Elliott divided her class into two groups: brown-eyed and blue-eyed. The first day one group got favored treatment and the other was discriminated against. On the second day the roles were reversed, and the third day the class discussed what they had

---

7. Reinhold Niebuhr, The Nature and Destiny of Man (New York: Charles Scribner's Sons, 1953), 1:166.
8. Hans Küng, On Being a Christian (Garden City, N.Y.: Doubleday and Company, 1976), 76.

learned. Ms. Elliott found that each day the favored group did better on their school work, and that after the experiment both groups did better. The children learned the meaning of prejudice, and because of the three-day experiment they related to each other in a new way.

The second documentary was a follow-up. Ms. Elliott had not only repeated the experiment in her classes each year; she had also developed race-relations seminars and teacher-training programs to teach her methods to others. The second film also included interviews with the former students who had been in Ms. Elliott's class when the first film was made. Their responses showed that the experiment had meant more to them than most other learning experiences in their lives. As parents they were now teaching their children the value of inclusiveness.

Jane Elliott is a Lutheran layperson who is living out her partnership with God. She had thought about her educational experiment for some time, and King's death gave her the incentive for trying it. She had no idea how it would turn out. She had no guarantee of what the results might be, either for her or for the students. She merely acted out of faith, with love, in the hope that she would be doing good.

Ms. Elliott was being a partner with God in the best sense of the word. Her clarity about who she was became the source of her strength as she decided what to do in her daily workplace. She did what she could where she was. Her work touched the lives of others in a way that turned out to be important for them and eventually spread to others. Many people are better off because of what Jane Elliott did, and the world is closer to God's promise, all because she acted as God's partner at the time and place to which only she had access. Jane Elliott's story is concrete evidence of how God's promise of "a new heaven and a new earth" can be fulfilled in everyday life when someone claims his or her true identity as God's partner.

When you ask, "Who am I?" God answers, "You are my partner." It is your invitation to a life of hope.

Questions for Reflection

1. Do you often think about the questions Stan poses at the beginning of this chapter? How would most of your friends react if

you asked them how they felt about such questions? (Or how do they react, if you have asked them?)

2. If you are active in a church, do you often hear your deepest concerns addressed there in a helpful way? If not, how might you help your church to address them more effectively?

3. How do you feel about being told that God wants you as a partner? How could knowing you were God's partner affect your everyday life in your home and your workplace? How might it let you reach out to others in new ways?

4. Do you agree that no task is too trivial for God's partners? What makes a task trivial?

5. How could you reexamine your understanding of what God wants you to be doing? How might you help others reexamine theirs? How might the church help its members do this regularly?

6. What other feelings or insights came to you as you read this part of the chapter about the question "Who am I?" and about being God's partner?

Who Am I?

Barbara: I Want to Be Somebody but I'm Afraid I'm Nobody

Who am I? I used to think this was a silly question because the answer seemed so obvious. I knew my name and address, what I looked like, what family and other groups I belonged to, what I was currently doing and what I had done in the past, and what talents and personality traits I had. Those facts seemed to make up a complete picture of me. What else could there be to say about who I was?

Rather than wondering who I was, I wondered why theologians, philosophers, and psychologists so often said that this was such an urgent question for everyone. Claiming that a question is unimportant is a common way of avoiding an answer that we don't want to hear. If I suspect that I'm a bad person or a worthless person, then I'd rather not even think about the question "Who am I?" Telling myself that the question is ridiculous is a lot more comfortable than trying to answer it. It's easier, too.

For this reason, many of us leave life's most important questions unasked for a long time. The questions are deep inside us, but we keep them buried so we won't have to face them. We cover them up with the busyness of daily life, or we disguise them in ways that let us avoid recognizing them.

Our personality types affect our ways of dealing with questions about who we really are and what life is all about. Avoiding these questions can be especially easy for extroverts. For them, the outer world of things and people has a strong attraction, and looking inward is an unpleasant chore. Extroverts are riskers and explorers in the outer world, but when it comes to the inner world they'd rather not look under any rocks to find out what might be underneath. Introverts are more likely to examine their thoughts and feelings and to ask penetrating questions about life's meaning, but even introverts find it hard to see themselves as they really are.

Whether we're introverts or extroverts, taking an honest look at ourseles can be scary. It's more comfortable to look only at our outward circumstances and at other people. Then we can blame them for our shortcomings and for whatever we're unhappy about, or we can enjoy feeling superior to them. So we all tend to avoid asking life's deepest questions. We just don't all do it in the same way.

Often we do it by giving pat answers that we know deep down aren't really answers. People ask "How are you?" and we answer "Fine!" rather than admitting that we're not fine at all. Or we do the opposite and dump all our current complaints on everyone who happens to cross our path. One acquaintance of mine uses this method regularly, and I dread running into her. I see her only once or twice a year, usually at the grocery store or at a crowded social event. I say, "Hi! How are you?" and try to keep moving. But she verbally pins me to the wall with a detailed report of her latest surgery and the ensuing complications, or the current problems of one of her grown children, whom I never knew well and haven't seen in years.

All these can be ways of avoiding the real questions about life's meaning. We avoid them when we're afraid we can't bear to learn the answers.

Sometimes the questions get harder to avoid

Every now and then, life forces us to ask one of the questions that we've been avoiding. Something happens that jolts us loose from our comfortable oblivion. A life-threatening illness strikes, a job or a marriage ends, or we arrive at a new stage of life and find that our former ways of coping no longer work. Then, if we let ourselves look honestly at what is happening, God begins showing us surprising answers to our questions.

Midlife was the jolt that got my attention. As I began seeing my life from a different perspective then, I also saw the question "Who am I?" in a new light. I still thought the answer was obvious, but it was a different answer from the one that had seemed obvious to me in earlier years. Instead of a collection of information—my name, address, and other such facts—my new answer was a collection of

painful feelings. I had finished the jobs that I felt society had assigned to me, I couldn't see anything that would replace them, and it
hurt.

Earlier in life I had graduated from college and then worked as a
mathematician for several years, but when I married, I quit my job
because I thought that was what all women were supposed to do. By
midlife, however, the job of full-time wife, mother, and community
volunteer no longer seemed enough. My daughter had graduated
from college, so she was no longer producing academic accomplishments that I could use as evidence of my success as a mother, and
she no longer needed the kind of personal services I had provided in
earlier years. I had been president of the community volunteer organizations that interested me, and now I was only a has-been in them.
I no longer had anything to do that provided a challenge or visible
results.

When I asked myself "Who am I?" my answer was "I'm nobody.
I'm not accomplishing anything. I'm not even working toward anything. I'm valuable only to my family members, and I'm valuable to
them only because I do the mindless background chores that keep
them comfortable and leave them free to use their time for better
things."

Most of what I was doing was routine household maintenance. I
picked up the newspapers and magazines and junk mail after family
members had laid them aside. I dusted and ran the vacuum cleaner.
I watered the houseplants and turned on sprinklers in the yard. I
gathered up our dirty clothes, ran them through the washer and
dryer, and returned them to the proper drawers and closets ready to
wear. I took clothing to the cleaners and picked it up when it was
ready. I did the grocery shopping and prepared meals. I sent cards
and notes and bought and wrapped gifts for our friends and relatives
when birthdays, weddings, and Christmas came around. Occasionally I went to lunch with women friends, or to traditional women's
parties honoring brides. Sometimes I had groups of friends over for
dinner. And I did the traditional volunteer jobs in my local church.

I knew I was capable of something very different. All my jobs
could be handled by almost any live, willing, available person, I felt.
None of them needed me or my talents specifically, and none of
them had any lasting results or moved me forward in any way. In
contrast to jobs in the outer world, in which one steadily becomes
more expert and is gradually given greater responsibility and

greater challenge, the home and church jobs I was doing kept me in the same place no matter how long I'd been doing them. These are the background-support jobs that our society has traditionally expected women to fill in their homes, churches, and communities. They're the jobs that everyone wants done but nobody wants to do.

When I began to take a fresh look at myself and at the circumstances in which I found myself at midlife, I felt hurt and angry about having nothing to do but these mindless jobs. My male contemporaries and even a few daring female ones had become the leaders of the business, professional, religious, and political world around me, but I had become a nobody, and it hurt.

What hurt most was knowing that I was just as capable as most of the people who were out there doing the things that I wanted to do and that society valued. I couldn't see why I should be stuck with doing the background-support jobs for other people, just so they could be free to do the things that used their talents and matched their interests. I couldn't see why my talents and interests were any less important than theirs.

I want to be a partner of some human beings

When I feel like a nobody I don't find much consolation in being told that my value comes only from being God's partner rather than from anything I do, so I see this issue a little differently from Stan.

No one can ever do enough to satisfy the hunger for achievement, much less to earn God's favor. But when someone who has had the opportunity to use his or her talents points this out to someone who hasn't, it's like a rich person telling a poor person that money is unimportant. Money *is* unimportant in one sense, and so is human achievement, but that doesn't justify giving only certain people access to these worldly rewards. Each person needs the opportunity to make his or her own choice about which rewards to work for.

If I haven't had the chance to do my best or to have it recognized and appreciated, the only thing that will make me feel valuable is for *human beings* to acknowledge my abilities and interests and to let me put them to full use. God seems vague and remote compared to the people who surround me in daily life, and it's hard for me to believe that God values me if I can't see that anyone else does.

Besides, I can't get very excited about knowing that God values everyone equally. If God had only a few partners and I was chosen to be one of them, I'd certainly consider that an important assignment. But if every other human being is God's partner too, then being God's partner doesn't seem like any big deal.

When I'm told that everyone is God's partner, I feel like the citizens of Venice in Gilbert and Sullivan's comic operetta *The Gondoliers*. In it, two Venetian gondoliers are unexpectedly made kings. They've always wished kings would treat their subjects as equals, so they put that policy into effect immediately. This new system sounds great to the Venetians at first, but then they see that there's a catch to it. "When everyone is somebody," they realize, "then no one's anybody!"

As the gondoliers-turned-kings found, equality isn't necessarily what we want, even though it sounds good at first. If equality means uniformity, it's not very appealing. Rather than uniformity, we want recognition for our unique qualities—for what lets us stand out from the crowd. If no one is any more valuable than anyone else, there's a sense in which we're all valueless. We're all nobodies.

So I'd like to be recognized for the things that I can do unusually well. I want to be appreciated for the things I have done that other people haven't done. I'm glad that God recognizes me as valuable just for existing, but that's not enough. I also want to be valued by other human beings, and I want to be valued for having something unique to offer.

If partnership with God is not reserved for special persons I don't find it particularly attractive, because I'm looking for something that is reserved for a special person—for me. I want to know that I'm not just an interchangeable part in a huge cosmic machine. Unless I think I belong on the bottom, equality is bad news

It seems to me that the only person who could get excited about being valued equally with every other human being, just for existing, would be the person who feels that he or she has no talents or resources that anyone needs. On the basis of the world's standards of measurement, this person has been assigned permanently to the bottom. The news that God uses a different standard and classifies everyone as equal would be great news to this person, like getting an unexpected promotion.

However, if I know that I have talents and other useful resources, I want the opportunity to use them, and I want my effectiveness in using them to be confirmed by the people around me. I want an assignment that another person couldn't handle but that I could. I want a job that challenges me to do my best, and when I've done it I want other people to acknowledge that I have done something worthwhile and done it well. Being told instead that I'm only valued the same as every other human being, including those who have refused to do anything with their abilities, seems like being given an unjustified demotion, and that's not good news at all.

Does God need *me*, or will just any live body do?

Isn't there a difference between the value we all have in God's sight, unrelated to anything that we do or fail to do, and the value that *does* relate to what we do—that comes from putting our unique collection of God-given resources to good use? Jesus talked about the importance of using one's talents fully, making them as productive as possible, rather than burying them (Matthew 25:14-30). He also said bearing good fruit was important (Matthew 7:17-20; Luke 3:9, 6:43, 13:6-8; John 15:1-8). He didn't say that God valued every tree equally; in fact, Jesus once cursed a tree for being fruitless (Matthew 21:19; Mark 11:13-14). There must be some sense in which God values what I do, in addition to valuing me just because I exist.

If, as Stan says, I "must be busy with the right things," am I not more valuable in some sense when I do "the right things" than when I do the wrong ones or do nothing? Isn't there any sense in which a person who doesn't kill anyone is more valuable than a mass murderer, even though in another sense God values the mass murderer just as much as anyone else? Wouldn't God value a person's use of his or her talent to discover the cure for a serious disease, in contrast to letting that talent stay unused?

What I know, what I can do, and what I choose to do contribute to making me the particular person that I am, so I can't believe they're unimportant. Of course part of what I know and can do is the result of innate God-given abilities, and part is due to circumstances that I did not cause or even choose. But even though I can't take any credit for these, they contribute to making me the particular individual that I am. They make me able to do some things that someone with different abilities and experiences couldn't do.

In addition to what I know and can do through no effort or choice of my own, however, I know some things because I've made a deliberate effort to find them out, and I can do some things because I've deliberately learned to do them. I've done some things by choice. Doesn't God value my having chosen these instead of something else? Am I wrong in wanting human beings to value that too? To me, Jesus' parable about talents seems to say that God values what each person does with her or his unique collection of God-given talents, in addition to valuing that person just for being a person. God has invested certain qualities in me, and I am partly responsible for the return that is realized from that investment, so God must value my accepting that responsibility and acting on it.

Being told that because I'm God's partner I should be satisfied with merely preparing my family's meals and cleaning the house and doing the laundry and running all the day-to-day errands for my family is discouraging, if I can do other things that the wider world needs and that use my talents more fully. And being told that I'm a full partner in the church feels like a put-down if I'm only allowed to do the church's menial background jobs but am willing and able to do more. It's a Pollyanna answer, a pair of rose-colored glasses to keep me from noticing that my main talents have been buried and that I've been unjustly classified as an inferior person.

I think a task that leaves many of my God-given capabilities unused and that keeps me from undertaking a larger task to which God calls me *is* trivial. I know that God is with me when I'm washing dishes, and if that's the job that uses my talents best and God wants me to do, it's not trivial. But if God has called me to something else and I'm washing dishes instead of doing that something else, then washing dishes is trivial and I'm using it as a way of avoiding God's call.

Some contemporary Christians have suggested that the sin to which women are most susceptible is triviality, rather than the pride or covetousness that male theologians over the centuries have often called the basic sins that underlie all others. Women have traditionally been required to be humble, subservient, and selfless while men have been encouraged to be confident, assertive initiative-takers. Women, therefore, tend to sin by failing to use their abilities or even to acknowledge that they have any, rather than by overestimating their own importance. Many women have become satisfied with doing only trivial things, because these have so often been the only things that society has let them do.

If I am God's partner, I need to get busy doing the particular tasks that God has equipped me for and called me to do. I can't be satisfied with merely doing whatever tasks happen to fill my time and meet other people's expectations.

Some Christians say, "Bloom where you are planted," but I'm afraid following this policy is often a cop-out, a rationalization, a way of avoiding God's call. God often wants to transplant people!

What if God is calling you to bloom more fully, in a place where your blooms can benefit more people? What if Abraham and Sarah had responded to God's call (Genesis 12:1-6) by saying, "No, thanks, God. We know you're with us in whatever we do, and no task is too trivial, so we'll just bloom right here where you first planted us. We'll stay here and do a good job of tending our flocks rather than striking out to lead our group toward a promised land"?

I think God has a unique spot for me to fill, a spot that only I can fill. I think that in some way God says to each person, "I need *you* for this particular job. I need someone in the position you are in to reach the people only you can reach. I need *you*, made up of the unique combination of talents I have given you plus what you have contributed toward their development." I don't think God says, "I need whatever live body happens to be willing and available, and you'll do."

God assigns some tasks to all people—tasks like going into all the world and communicating the gospel, and loving our neighbors. But when it comes to the specifics—going into a certain part of the world and communicating a particular part of the gospel in a particular way to some particular people at a particular time, or showing love in a specific way to a specific person at a specific time and place—I believe God assigns unique tasks to each of us. I believe that being God's partner means finding out what my particular assignment is and then getting busy carrying it out, using the particular combination of abilities that I have.

God seems to have deliberately set up the world in a way that leaves blanks for human beings to fill. God evidently has chosen to leave some things undone rather than to do everything that needs doing. We humans complete God's creation and serve as God's partners by doing our assigned parts, by filling in the particular blanks that God has left for us to fill. This means that something that needs doing goes undone when I fail to carry out my assignments.

Some Christians find this thought scary or even sinful, because it seems to deny the traditional picture of God as all-powerful. But the basic nature of God is community. Christians have always expressed that by speaking of God as a Trinity—three persons who interact and communicate with each other. And in community, no one person has everything that is needed for the good of the whole community. Each of us has different abilities and personality traits, and to form the whole that God has in mind they must be added together. So God evidently values not only the particular combination that God has given to each different individual, but also each individual's willingness to put his or her abilities at the disposal of the community in order to help complete God's creation.

If this is true—if what matters is what Stan calls "willingness to be a part of a larger community" and to "claim my identity as God's partner"—then doesn't that willingness contribute to my value in some way?

Can't we take turns being somebodies and nobodies?

Besides being God's partners, each of us also needs opportunities to be the partner of other human beings. This may in fact be the main way in which we act out our roles as God's partners. In our culture, however, non-white ethnic groups, women, and the poor have rarely been allowed into full partnership with their fellow human beings. Part of what Christian feminists and other contemporary Christian theologians are advocating is mutuality in relationships. This means taking turns, with one person taking the lead in one situation and a different person in another situation, based on who has the abilities that are needed in each situation.

If we took turns like this, each person would be a relative nobody at times, but he or she would get to be somebody at other times. This is very different from the traditional pattern of our churches and our society, in which certain groups are almost always the somebodies and others are always the nobodies. Part of the church's failure to carry out its mission effectively may come from its failure to be a network of human beings who are partners with each other as well as with God.

I suspect that God intends the church to be like a dynamic, living network of laypeople, women and men of all kinds, with clergy and other professionals stationed at key points to provide specialized help but changing their roles and locations as the network's needs change.

Instead of being this kind of flexible network of partners, most of our institutional churches have become rigid structures with a

fixed chain of command. God apparently wants the church's struc-
ture to be something like a wispy, bouncy spiderweb, but we've
made it like a huge, iron pyramid instead, with a few people permanently on top and many others permanently restricted to the lower
levels. Worst of all, we seem determined to keep it that way.

Our local congregations too often function like rimless wheels,
with the pastor as the center and the lay members as spokes that
have no connection to each other except through the center. In this
kind of system, members don't know each other's needs or abilities,
and they don't feel any obligation to work together. The spokes have
no support at the wheel's outer edge where they must meet the hard
pavement and stay firm. No wonder these wheels don't go very far!

Both the laity and clergy help to preserve this ineffective pattern. Most lay members want to deal directly with the pastor, not
with any lay intermediary or subordinate staff member. Being in
close touch with the central person is a sign of one's importance.
Pastors, often fearing that laypeople may criticize them and endan-
ger their job security, are reluctant to reveal their real thoughts and
feelings. And because they've often had laypeople fail to do assigned
jobs, they hesitate to delegate jobs. As a result, when we try to get
the wheel rolling, the few spokes on whom its weight rests soon col-
lapse or become distorted, and the center is pulled apart mercilessly.
Surely this isn't what God intends.

Who are we? We are all God's partners. Yet how can we become
partners with each other as well, giving each person the opportunity
to use his or her talents to the fullest and to be appreciated for doing
so, even in the church? None of us are God, but we aren't nobodies
either. The way we treat ourselves and other people needs to reflect
that, especially within the church.

Questions for Reflection

1. How often have you wondered who you really were? Has this
changed over the course of your life? If so, how?

2. Do you tend to "look under the rocks" in your life, or do you
prefer not to know what is underneath them? Which do you find
scarier: to examine your own thoughts, feelings, relationships, and
ways of functioning, or to risk and explore in the outer world?

3. What events in your life have jolted you into having to reconsider what was important, as midlife did for Barbara?

4. Do you feel like a "somebody"? If so, what contributes to that feeling? If not, what would have to change to make you feel like a "somebody" instead of a "nobody"?

5. How do you feel about God's wanting everyone for partners?

6. How does being equal differ from being alike? In what ways do you want to be considered the equal of everyone else? In what ways do you want to be recognized as different from others?

7. What particular task do you feel God has equipped you to do and calls you to do? Are you doing it? If not, what prevents you? How might you start doing it (or doing it more fully) now?

8. Do you think it is selfish to want to make full use of your main talents? Explain your response.

9. What value comes from your own efforts to develop your talents or acquire skills? What part do you think God expects you to play in this process?

10. How do you feel about the idea that God has deliberately left "blanks" for human beings to fill?

11. How could the church encourage and enable laypeople to use their God-given abilities more fully? How might you help your church to do what you are suggesting?

12. What other thoughts or feelings came to you as you read this part of the chapter about being God's partner?

Chapter 2

What Shall I Do?
Barbara: What Kind of Work Gets God's Stamp of Approval?

In my family, children's birthdays have always been big events. When my daughter was little, we spent days getting ready for her birthday each year. As an only child, my parents' only grandchild, and my in-laws' only granddaughter, she was the focus of much interest, so her first few birthdays were exciting times for our whole family.

I especially remember her second birthday. Well ahead of time, I invited relatives to come for a birthday dinner, and I started getting ready. First I made a detailed list of what needed to be done when. Then I got out the "good silver" and polished it. I pressed the rarely-used linen tablecloths. I planned a special meal and prepared parts of it in advance, including making and decorating a birthday cake.

Early on the big day I set tables with our best silver and china and arranged flowers from the yard for centerpieces. That afternoon my parents arrived from out of town, bringing their carefully wrapped gifts and great excitement.

As party time approached, preparations sped up and the excitement intensified. We all dressed in our party clothes and then rushed around the house making sure that everything was ready. Soon the guests began arriving. I was busy in the kitchen, putting the finishing touches on the meal and seeing that every dish emerged from the oven or refrigerator at exactly the right time. Right on schedule, everything was ready. Everything on my list had been checked off, and it was time to serve dinner.

Then we realized that someone was missing. My mother-in-law had not arrived, and we felt we couldn't start without her. We waited. The hot foods began getting cold, and the cold foods warm. I put them back into the oven and refrigerator in an effort to salvage them. My daughter began getting fretful, as it was now past her usual mealtime and getting close to her bedtime. Waiting to eat and to open her presents was getting harder and harder, but her grandmother, who lived only a few blocks away, still hadn't come. Finally we decided to go ahead and eat. About halfway through the meal our missing guest arrived, looking harried. She had come straight from the hospital, she explained, without taking time to go by home and change clothes or comb her hair, and she hadn't found time to wrap her birthday gift so she had brought it in a brown paper grocery sack.

While visiting a hospitalized friend during the afternoon, she told us, she had come across a woman from out of town whose husband was a patient and was seriously ill. My mother-in-law felt the woman needed someone to keep her company, so she sat with her. She was sorry to be late for the party, she assured us, but she was sure we understood that this woman needed her. I wasn't sure that I did.

Are family obligations God's first priority?

Which work is God's work in a situation like this? When a Christian is confronted with conflicting demands on his or her time, how should he or she decide which one to respond to?

Maybe caring for family members should take first priority. After all, I'm my daughter's only mother and my husband's only wife. I also happen to be my parents' only child. Surely this gives me a greater responsibility toward these family members than toward the people outside my family circle.

Could we use this standard for solving the problem of the birthday party? Hundreds of people were at the hospital that day, and few of them were due at their only granddaughter's second birthday party. My mother-in-law was the only person who could fill her role in her family, but any one of a number of people could have sat with the hospital patient's wife.

Church members often use this standard for deciding whether to participate in church activities. They say they can't come to a Bible study because it meets at the time when they need to take their children to soccer practice. They can't be in the choir because on re-hearsal nights they need to be at home seeing that their children do their homework. They can't come to church programs on Sunday afternoons or evenings, they say, because that's the only time for doing things together as a family, and that has to be their first priority.

Does it? In these times when family life is under attack from all sides, Christians tend to defend it by giving family activities first priority, and on the surface this seems admirable. But it may not be God's priority for us. Surprising as it may seem, the Bible doesn't put much emphasis on loyalty to one's family. In fact, the Gospels often show Jesus downplaying the importance of family obligations.

Once Jesus told a big crowd what was required of his disciples. He said, "If anyone comes to me and does not hate his father and mother, his wife and children, his brothers and sisters—yes, even his own life—he cannot be my disciple" (Luke 14:26, NIV). On another occasion he said he came to cause division, not harmony, within families (Luke 12:49-53).

Most of us would consider a parent's death an occasion when family obligations would certainly come before all others, but Jesus evidently didn't see it that way at all. He wouldn't let a potential follower go and bury his father before joining Jesus. And on another occasion, Jesus wouldn't even let a man take time to go back and tell his family good-bye (Luke 9:59-62).

Just as Jesus didn't let his followers give family obligations first priority, he didn't seem to give top priority to his own biological family. Once when he was speaking to a crowd, someone came and told him, "Your mother and brothers are standing outside, wanting to see you." He didn't rush to see what they wanted. He didn't even say, "Tell them I'll come just as soon as I finish this sermon." Instead, he acted as if he had no special attachment to them at all. "My mother and brothers," he said, "are those who hear God's word and put it into practice" (Luke 8:19-21, NIV).

If our unique obligations to our immediate families don't have first call on our time, what does? Maybe our first priority should be whatever job has the most pressing time deadline, compared to those that can be done just as well at a later time. Couldn't my mother-in-law have come to the birthday party on time and then gone back later to sit with the patient's wife again? Then she could have done both things.

Where does carrying out a commitment fit in? Doesn't God want us to do what we promise to do, even if something we'd rather do is offered later? Wasn't it wrong for my mother-in-law to break her promise to be at the family dinner at a certain time, even if she considered what came along later more important?

Should the relative seriousness of the needs be our basis for deciding which need to respond to when we're faced with several legitimate ones? Medical personnel call this method triage: when they can't treat everyone immediately, they start with the people who have the most serious wounds but seem able to be saved. Recognizing which needs we can meet is usually not too hard, so maybe we could use the triage method if we could decide which ones were most deserving. That sounds easy enough, but it isn't always.

A two-year-old's birthday party may not seem very important in the overall scheme of things. What the guests wear, whether the gifts are beautifully wrapped, and whether the food is served in ideal condition are undoubtedly trivial problems compared to those many people in the world face, like not having any clothes to wear or anything to eat. Maybe birthday parties are also trivial compared to sitting with a sick man's wife who is alone far from home.

On the other hand, for a two-year-old, a birthday is a major event. Dressing up and getting special surprises that come from pretty wrappings are a big part of the excitement. Family members are the main people in a two-year-old's life, and feeling important to them has a long-lasting effect on a child's self-confidence.

Both laity and clergy have hard choices to make

Dilemmas like this, as well as much more serious ones, arise constantly. Clergy, for example, are always having to choose between fulfilling obligations to their own families and going to the aid of others. Church members usually expect their pastor to come at once when crises occur in their lives, without regard for the pastor's other commitments. Many church members even expect their pastor to be immediately available for trivial purposes that could easily wait until a more convenient time or even be left undone. As a result, spouses and children of clergy are often left alone at crucial times because the clergyperson is away attending a church meeting or dealing with a church member's problems. And clergy suffer from frustration and burnout because they can't meet all of their members' expectations, to say nothing of meeting those of their own families and themselves.

Laypersons in helping professions or service-oriented jobs often find themselves facing the same kind of dilemma. And aren't they doing God's work too, even though they don't do it through the institutional church? What about the doctor on call, who has to leave an important family event to rush to the bedside of a patient? Or the electric company employee who is called to restore power when a storm hits?

People who enter these kinds of careers know what to expect, and of course they're being paid to perform these services. Also, these professional helpers often work in groups and can therefore take turns being on call. But even if some of our service to others is scheduled and paid for, we're still confronted by needs that go beyond what we thought we were enlisted to do.

What about the work that comes along unexpectedly, that seems to be beyond the call of duty? How do we know when God is calling us to a higher duty, one that justifies—even requires—laying our routine obligations aside and trying to be God's person outside of our usual working hours, or outside of our usual circle of family, friends, and job?

Is church work always God's work?

What kind of work does God want us to do? Work in the institutional church? Work that provides monetary income? Work that meets our family members' needs? Work that helps other people in need? It's a hard question, and it's easy to delude ourselves about why we choose some ways of using our time and talents and refuse others.

It's deceptively easy, for example, to use family obligations as an excuse for not doing other things that we don't want to do. After all, surely no one can say that our duty to our family is unimportant. We conveniently overlook what Jesus said about it, and also we often overlook the fact that we often give up time that we could spend with our family in order to do other things we'd rather do. It looks a little suspicious when we use family obligations as our reason for being unavailable for church activities but we readily leave our families to go to entertainment or social events.

But being church-sponsored doesn't automatically make something God's work. Churches are made up of human beings, and not every program they plan is something that God wants done. And even if a certain program is something God wants done, it may not be what God is calling *me* to do.

In the church, just as in any other organization, active members can easily come to see the organization and its administrative functions as ends in themselves, and as the most important thing for everyone to do. In the church this may be a special danger for clergy and other church employees, since they depend on the church for their livelihood and spend so much of their time in church-sponsored activities. But it is also a problem for active volunteers in the church who too often assume that religious activities are automatically more God's work than "secular" activities.

Some of what we think of as secular activities may in fact be what God cares about most. We're still the church when we're doing these things, but we tend to lose sight of that. God calls each Christian to some kind of ministry, but we'd rather not think about that. It's easier to assume that all ministry is supposed to be done by clergy and that what we do is second-class Christian work compared to the work that clergy do. We assume that the most committed Christians become clergy and the rest of us remain laity because we want an easier, halfhearted way.

Many of us *have* chosen a halfhearted way, and we're *not* always willing to do what God is calling us to do, but the evidence of that is not our failure to become priests or pastors of churches. It's our failure to be the best parent, business owner, laborer, or artist that we can be. We refuse to acknowledge, develop, and use our main talents, whatever they may be. We do not allow God to make contact with us and help us find out what God is calling us to do. Most of all, we fail to put ourselves at God's disposal as we go about our daily lives, whatever they may include.

Clergy (who do their daily work as agents of the institutional church) and laypeople (most of whom do not) are equally accountable to God for doing the jobs that God assigns to them. God expects both groups to do ministry, but not the same ministry. Neither group has a monopoly on doing God's work or failing to do it.

God calls us to be a community

When we're out in the world doing our daily jobs as lay men and women, we're being what has traditionally been called "the scattered church," in contrast to "the gathered church" that meets for worship on Sunday mornings and for other purposes at other times. But if this is true, why bother to be part of the gathered church? Why not just stay scattered all the time? Why should we feel any obligation to meet with other Christians for worship, or to work with them on church-sponsored projects? Why should churches complain about members who work diligently in the Lions Club or the Junior League or the hospital auxiliary and yet refuse to accept jobs in the church? Why be concerned about church members who don't support their churches but who give large amounts of their time and money to other organizations? Why worry about the people who just watch sermons on television on Sunday mornings instead of attending a local church?

We need the gathered church because people who are always scattered soon stop being a group, and a group is stronger than any individual working alone. For a church to be effective, its members must gather regularly and be involved in some group efforts. They can't just be out doing their own things separately and still be the kind of community that God calls the church to be.

Our gatherings give us a chance to find each other so we can join forces for more effective ministry than any one of us could do alone. Gathered, we can learn what each other's talents are, and we can help each other develop those talents so that they can be used to best advantage in the work God calls each person to do.

Our gatherings also teach new Christians what being a Christian means. Our gatherings help experienced Christians grow in faith through their interaction with others. We can discover more of God by hearing how others have experienced God. And we can each become more Christlike if we come together regularly to hold each other accountable for the disciplined living that God asks of us.

If we refuse to help make these functions available for the gathered church, the church will die, so we can't just stay scattered if we want it to live. What we know as "church work" isn't automatically God's work, and it's nowhere near *all* of God's work, but some of it is a necessary part of God's work.

Of course we can't stay gathered all the time, either, and expect to get God's work done. God doesn't intend our gatherings to be ends in themselves. We can't go back to the days when local churches were the source of most social activities and community service, because the world has changed since then.

God calls us to minister to *today's world*: not to yesterday's world, and not just to our own little circle of family, friends, and acquaintances. The church isn't intended to be merely a safe, unchanging refuge for its members. We can't just stay in our own

comfortable familiar groups and expect the world to come to us for
what we want to give.

A lot of God's work requires getting out among non-church
members, meeting them on their own ground, speaking their language, finding out what their real concerns and needs are, and then
ministering to them. That's evidently what God intends our gatherings to prepare us for.

So we do need to gather, and each of us must take part of the
responsibility for our gatherings, but we also need to scatter. God's
work is out there in the world waiting for us, and we are the people
God calls to do it. The main job of the clergy is to train, fortify, and
organize us laypeople for carrying out our God-given assignments.
It's not to do those assignments for us.

What keeps laypeople from doing their God-given ministries?

Sometimes we refuse our assignments and expect the clergy to
do them for us, but sometimes the clergy are unwilling to *let* laypeople do real ministry. Unfortunately, over the last several centuries
we've developed an unhealthy relationship between clergy and laity
in the church. Clergy too often fill all of the leadership roles and
require laypeople to stay in the background-support roles. This pattern sadly resembles our society's pattern of keeping men in dominant roles and requiring women to stay in subservient ones. It's also
the same pattern that has kept white people dominant and non-
whites subservient.

This sharp distinction between clergy and laity didn't exist when
the church began, and it clearly isn't what God intends, just as the
larger pattern of dominance and subservience isn't what God intends for society as a whole.

Sad to say, there are many ways in which this pattern encourages Christians to leave their God-given talents unused and their
God-assigned ministries undone. For one thing, the church's separation of laity and clergy, combined with society's separation of the
roles of men and women, keep many lay Christians as passive followers when God is calling them to be leaders.

We have come to see the spiritual leadership of the church as
the exclusive province of the clergy, and the business leadership as
the province of the laity. We therefore rarely allow laypeople to
speak publicly about subjects like theology and biblical interpretation, or to give spiritual guidance. Because these are the jobs we

reserve for clergy, laypeople whose talents and interests are in these areas have a hard time finding outlets for their abilities even though they are badly needed in the church and the world.

Also, until very recent years our society has allowed only men to be its leaders in business, government, and most professions. So when our churches need members to take charge of "worldly" areas like finance and property ownership and dealings with political leaders, we usually call on men. This system has too often left women with nothing to do in their churches except jobs like cooking, telephoning, visiting sick and elderly members, and teaching the children. Women whose abilities and interests lie elsewhere have few opportunities to use them.

Because continuing this pattern seems easier and more comfortable than changing it, many keep trying to stifle everyone who wants the church to change. Those critical, rabble-rousing troublemakers should just quiet down and stop trying to rock the boat. After all, we keep telling ourselves, this system has worked okay for centuries.

If we keep everything just as it is, perhaps we can avoid seeing our churches disrupted by controversy. Clergy can rest secure in their positions as the unquestioned experts on the Bible and theology and the Christian life, and lay businessmen can enjoy being the unquestioned financial decision-makers for the church. The dangers of letting men and women who aren't married to each other work as colleagues can be avoided. If we stick to the old system, we keep thinking, there won't be any uncertainty about who belongs where, and no one will be tempted to step outside the bounds of what is proper.

But God knows us better than that, and God seems to have something different in mind.

God calls us to change

We may see no reason to change the present pattern if we happen to be among the people who have opportunities to use our talents within it. Even if our greatest talents are going unused, we may feel fine about continuing the present pattern, since for centuries we have been told that ignoring our abilities and staying meekly in the background are virtuous ways of behaving—Christian ways, in fact. Women, especially, have been admonished that God wants us to be submissive at all times. We've been deluded into thinking that it's an honor to be kept on a pedestal, admired for our appearance and our childlike innocence and protected from the dangers of the wider world.

Now God is nudging us to realize how damaging this pattern really is, not only for those who have been kept subservient but also for those who have traditionally had exclusive rights to the dominant positions in our churches and our society. God is also showing us that temptations are always present when men and women work together, but that harm can also come from not letting them do so. We can't avoid danger by frantically trying to keep men and women separate in their daily jobs. Our only hope is to begin replacing the harmful pattern of dominance-subservience with one of mutuality in relationships.

The Bible says a lot about this better pattern that God is trying to move us toward. In terms of the church and society as a whole, it's called community. In terms of relationships between individuals, it's called love.

When we try to identify God's work in our churches and our world, we meet other problems besides this one of dominance and subservience. We also run into trouble because of the distinction our society makes between lay and professional people in all fields. In earlier years this was not such a problem, but most work has now become specialized and highly skilled, based on information rather than on physical effort or on making things. We now want many jobs done by professional people who have had a specific course of formal education and who have a set of officially approved credentials. So if we are not clergy and not a credentialed professional who gets paid for doing what we do, we're likely to be rejected on two counts when we try to find places to do the work that God calls us to do as Christians.

Finding this rejection in our churches is especially sad, because it's a sharp contrast to the way the Bible portrays the church: a community of faith in which every member has God-given abilities that he or she is called to use in ministering to others. Even our language reflects our neglect of what God intends for the church and its ministry. We too often speak of "ministers" when we actually mean "clergy." God calls every Christian to be a minister, but God doesn't call us all to be clergy.

It looks as if we're back to square one in our efforts to identify God's work. Family duties don't always qualify, and religious work—

the work that clergy and laity do within the institutional church—doesn't seem to, either. What does?

Is meeting human needs God's work?

Maybe God's work is any work that involves caring for other people and meeting their needs, in contrast to work that merely meets our own needs. But should the needs of others and the world always come before our own? If we accept this as our standard, how will we carry out Jesus' command to love others as we love ourselves? Loving ourselves seems to be a necessary part of obeying this commandment. Neglecting or mistreating ourselves keeps us from being able to meet others' needs effectively.

Accepting this fact is often especially hard for women, because traditionally we've been trained and expected to put others first at all times. Many women, especially Christian women, feel that it's okay to think of themselves and do things for their own enjoyment, but only after everyone else's needs and expectations have been met. This often means never. The women's movement of recent years has rightly pointed out that always putting the needs of others first can be an oppressive and unjust burden even when on the surface it looks like admirable Christian self-sacrifice. Self-sacrifice is Christlike only when it is freely chosen, not when it is forced on us.

Recent findings about addiction and the dangers of codependence have also helped us see that meeting others' needs can be a dangerous trap. As many family members of alcoholics and other addicts have learned, meeting another person's every need can keep that person from taking responsibility for himself or herself. That kind of caregiving takes away the caregiver's self-worth while letting the addict avoid recovery. Each one is helping the other continue a damaging way of functioning, without seeing what is really happening. We find, then, that meeting needs of others without giving any attention to our own can be harmful to all concerned. So we can't assume that serving others is always God's work.

We also have to face the problem of choosing which needs to try to meet, out of the gigantic number that we know of. Each of us can do only so much, and it's hard to choose between all of the good causes that we could support, or the many people who need the kind of help that we're able to give. The needs seem so overwhelming, and the possibility of meeting them so small, that we're tempted to give up and not even try.

If God's work involves trying to meet the needs of others, how can we distinguish real needs from mere wants? Doing everything another person wants you to do is not the same as doing what he or she needs. And yet, wants aren't necessarily bad, are they? Can't work that meets people's wants be God's work? I sometimes want to travel, to read, to attend operas and concerts, and to do various other things simply for enjoyment, and I don't think God disapproves of my doing them. If these and other kinds of things that people do for fun are not bad things, then tour guides, hotel operators, writers, composers, performers, and many other workers who provide enjoyment are doing some of God's work, too. Evidently, to come up with work that doesn't qualify as God's work we'll have to find something else besides work that merely meets people's wants.

What about something really lazy and frivolous like total escape from work? According to the Bible and Christian tradition, even God uses time for rest, so even idleness must be okay in its place.

Is all work God's work?

It seems that we're getting close to saying that all human activity is God's work. That can't be right, can it? What about work whose products damage their users' physical, mental, or spiritual health? What about activity that promotes gross extravagance in a world where physical hunger and homelessness are rampant? Can God's work include hosting or attending social events that require wearing clothes that cost thousands of dollars and will be worn only once or twice, even if the proceeds of such events go to charity? And what about work that encourages people to feel like outcasts if they aren't wearing the latest fad in clothing, or if they don't own expensive cars or stereo equipment, even when they can't afford necessities? Surely some kinds of work are not God's work, but where is the line?

Maybe whatever promotes human health and wholeness and is not harmful to anyone is God's work. We'll have to include promoting justice and the equitable distribution of what God provides, but surely with this category we're getting close to identifying the boundaries of God's work. Aren't we?

I'm afraid not. There's still a slight problem. As Stan has reminded us, we can't be sure what the outcome of our actions will be, so we can't always know whether our work will turn out to be helpful or harmful in the long run.

There's another problem, too. Some of us have a hard time seeing the value of the kind of work that other people do, because of our different talents and personality traits. Practical realists tend to see only the importance of work that provides life's physical necessities like food, clothing, and shelter. These sense-oriented people want to see concrete, measurable results from work. They put heavy emphasis on the physical products and monetary income that work furnishes.

In contrast, others of us are oriented to creative, theoretical, or artistic work. We see the need for brainstorming, envisioning, experimenting, and many forms of expression, and we're good at doing those things. We know that some valuable products of work are mental and spiritual rather than physical. Such products often don't become apparent until long after the work is done, yet they make valuable contributions to human life.

Both of these kinds of work and their products are essential for what the Bible calls abundant life—for the kind of total health and full flowering of our abilities that God evidently wants for each of us. But it's easy to think that only the kind of work we ourselves do is important, and that what others do is either too frivolous or too ordinary to be worthwhile.

Besides having a hard time seeing that all kinds of work, not just the kinds we ourselves do best, are needed, some of us have a hard time being satisfied with what we have chosen to do after we've chosen it. Especially when our efforts don't turn out perfectly (which, for everyone, is most of the time), we're tempted to re-hash our decisions and to think we should have chosen something different. Then the next time we're confronted with more than one thing that needs doing, we're paralyzed into doing nothing, for fear of making a choice we'll regret later.

Sin bravely, and thank God for grace

Plenty of difficulties and dangers confront us when we try to choose the work that God wants us to do. But the greatest danger lies in thinking that finding the right work and doing it will earn God's stamp of approval. God's acceptance isn't based on the work we do, no matter what kind of work it is. We have God's acceptance already, even before we do anything. The Bible calls it grace.

It's hard to find a balance between being able to depend on God's grace to make our efforts fruitful, and needing to recognize God's work and do it well. Both are important. I guess we'll have to take Martin Luther's advice after all—to sin bravely. We'll have to plunge forward, doing the best we can with the work that presents itself to us but knowing that we will make mistakes.

Once we've done our best to choose our jobs and do them well, we'll have to depend on God to put our efforts to good use, whether the job is hosting a two-year-old's birthday party, sitting with a stranger at a hospital, or holding a top leadership position in the church or the world.

We'll have to count on God's grace, too, to cover what we've done in the past, before we had the insights we have now. We older women, for example, who stayed in subservient positions in the past can be confident that what we did was good, even if we now see good reasons for refusing to stay in those positions. And people who have followed the traditional path to what the world defined as success can still claim God's grace for what they have done, even if they now see that success isn't all that they expected it to be.

While claiming God's grace for our past we can also set out on new paths, even late in life. With God-given strength and confidence, we can risk doing new things that God calls us to do, although our culture and even our churches may oppose us.

When we face hard choices and think of embarking on daring new paths, it would help if we had a model of some kind—a real person who has actually done the kinds of things that we think God is calling us to do. It would also help to have a personal advisor right on the scene when an especially hard choice arises, to encourage us and remind us of the important things we need to consider. A hot line direct to God would be ideal.

God seems to have known we'd need those.

Questions for Reflection

1. How do you feel about Barbara's story of the birthday party? Which of her mother-in-law's obligations do you think was most important?

2. How do you think God wants you to choose what to do when you are confronted with several demands on your time? What kind of work or other activities should have top priority when you can't do it all?

3. What priority do you think God puts on your being available for your family's needs or wants, compared to doing other things you feel called to do? On what authority do you base your answer?

4. If you are active in a church, do you think work done in the name of the church should have top priority? On what authority do you base your answer?

5. If people are doing important, time-consuming work that helps others in their community but is not done under the direct sponsorship of the church, should this exempt them from the responsibility for doing their share of needed jobs within the church? What are your reasons for answering the way you do?

6. Should the church have lay volunteers as spiritual leaders, or should such jobs be done only by formally trained professionals with credentials? Should lay volunteers work in the church only as helpers for clergy and other church professionals? Why do you feel as you do?

7. Do you see the church keeping women in subservient roles? Does God want it this way? If not, how might you help to bring about change? Explain why you feel as you do.

8. When have you dared to do something that you felt God was calling you to do, and been opposed by your friends or co-workers or by your church? How did you respond?

9. What other feelings or thoughts came to you as you read Barbara's part of this chapter on work?

What Shall I Do?
Stan: God Has a Job in Mind for You

Every day you are expected to do the activities and tasks that you do well. You expect it of yourself, and you know that others expect it of you. You may often wonder, "Is my work good enough? Is my work better than other people's?"

As God's partner, you don't just wonder, "Will my work please others?" Instead, you want to know if you have done your best, and you may feel that somehow you could have done better. This presents you with a dilemma: What good is it to be God's partner if what you do doesn't measure up? The question can be discouraging, too, if you feel that your work must always be perfect.

These disturbing questions aren't new. They have bothered every sensitive person who has ever tried to live as God's partner or even seriously considered it. From time to time people have tried to find solutions to the dilemma that such questions present. Some people try giving up on doing good works in their everyday lives and doing them only in "spiritual" or "religious" contexts instead. This method is irresponsible because it avoids the call to be God's partners where we live daily.

Augustine of Hippo understood this responsibility to be God's partner in the real world. When the Vandals were about to cross the Straits of Gibraltar and Rome was in danger, Augustine was approached by a general in the Roman legion, who wanted to become a monk because his wife had died. "For God's sake, not now!" Augustine exclaimed. You can't be God's partner by refusing your worldly obligations.

Yet knowing this makes the dilemma worse. You can't turn away from your obligations to others who depend on you, but you feel that your work will never be good enough. And limiting yourself to religious work doesn't let you escape the problems, since they're found in all kinds of work, including religious.

So how can you be God's partner when you feel so inadequate for the job? Looking seriously at the disturbing questions can be the first step.

The world needs the work of God's partners

As God's partner, you know that good works are needed to keep the world from coming apart. The world runs as well as it does only because countless people do their routine daily jobs. No matter how well they do their work, they do it, day in and day out.

They have many different reasons for doing it. For some people work provides fulfillment, while for others it is merely a way of getting life's necessities. Whatever the reasons for working may be, work enables the world to survive day after day. Jobs must be done, so people must do them. And the law of life is to preserve life, so keeping the world alive is good work. It is godly work.

As God's partner, however, you see that the world's judgment about what work qualifies as good has to be based on some kind of standards. Unless there is a way to motivate people to meet minimum standards of some sort, the world's future is in serious danger. But much work is needed and there is never enough talent and commitment to do it all, so the world has to be satisfied with what is available. It has to depend more on the workers' self-interest than on their willingness to do good work just because it is good.

For this reason the world must find a way to make self-interest benefit the whole community. Capitalists try to regulate self-interest by preserving a free market, socialists by regulating the economy, and Marxists by giving all power to the state. Supporters of these different systems may argue about which is the best way of keeping self-interest in check, but they all agree that self-interest must be used in some way. Somehow the world has to harness self-interest and direct it toward the good of the community.

For this reason we have laws that favor the community over the individual. Even communities that give the individual great protection allow individual rights to have a lower priority in times of emergency in order to preserve the community. The community decides which behaviors to reward and which to punish based on what will help the community to survive, and laws express the decisions that the community has made.

From these observations you can see that both natural laws and laws established by human beings aim at setting standards of work that will serve the community as a whole. Work that falls short of these standards endangers not only the worker who does it but also the fabric of the social order. So the law encourages good work in two ways: by restraining us, and by guiding us.

The law serves as a restraint by defining the minimum standards that behavior must meet. These standards are developed out of the community's collective experience, to set limits on our freedom. But laws must be general enough to cover all aspects of life, so they have to be technical and abstract. They can define the minimum standards of good work, but they can't set any maximum requirements.

The law serves as a guide when it encourages certain actions by rewarding them or at least by making them exempt from punishment. Some of the hardest decisions for the human community to make are those concerning what happens when legal standards conflict with moral ones. Morally sensitive persons will say that merely being legally right does not necessarily make work qualify as good. Still, the law has to define what makes work qualify as legal, even if there is no way to agree on whether it is good.

Being a partner with God needn't keep you from accepting the use of law as a way of promoting minimum standards for good work and thus protecting the world from the most destructive human tendencies. As God's partner you recognize the human spirit's potential for catastrophe and accept the usefulness of having a legal definition of good works. But you also know that your works must be measured by other standards.

How can you measure your work?

Even though your work is not illegal, as God's partner you also want it to meet higher standards than just being legal. To be good rather than just legal, your work would have to measure up in five areas: motivation, intentions, execution, permanence, and eventual results.

Motivation. Why are you doing the work that you do? Does your motivation make the work good? Maybe you do your work because it uses your particular talents. Maybe you want the reward or recognition that it brings – monetary income, security, prestige, convenience, or any number of other things that a job can furnish.

Maybe you work to benefit people whom you think need and deserve your help – that ought to be a good enough motive to make your work good. That motive is sneaky, though. Even when your good works meet others' real needs, you may be doing the work mainly to keep others dependent on you, because you need to be needed. You may want the self-satisfaction that comes from serving others. The further you look into your own motives, the less sure you can be about your reasons for doing the "good works" that you do! Then, deep down inside, you may fear that if your motives are not perfect, your works will not qualify as good.

Intentions. Surely your motives don't have to be perfect, if your intentions are good. You undoubtedly intend to do good, or at least not to do harm. But measured by love, do your intentions go far enough?

It's easy to let your good intentions reach only to the edges of your own personal circle of family, friends, and acquaintances – the people who are pretty much like you. Surely this isn't bad. After all, you can't help everyone, and aren't God's partners to do what they can in the places where they find themselves? True, but this fact can easily be used as an escape and a mere rationalization. You may need to expand the scope of your good intentions in order for your works to qualify as good.

Execution. Peter Drucker, the business management expert, likes to say that "everything degenerates into work." Even good motives and intentions are worthless if you don't act on them.

As soon as you act, you face the question of how well you are doing what you are doing. The quality of your work matters, not just to you but also to other people. You want to be proud of your work, and your standards usually get higher as your work gets better. It may never be as good as you want it to be, even if by the world's standards your work is outstanding. We see an example of this in Peter Shaffer's musical drama *Amadeus*. Near the end of a unique career of composing brilliant music, Mozart declares, "I've written nothing finally good!"[1]

---

1. Peter Shaffer, *Amadeus* (New York: Harper and Row, 1980), 87.

Even though your abilities are probably nowhere near as out-standing as Mozart's, you still tend to measure your work by a pic-ture of perfection that you can never match. By this standard you find it hard to call your works good.

Permanence. Another standard that you may think about in evaluating your work is its permanence. Will what you do last, or is it something that is useful only for the moment and has to be re-peated constantly? All work has some kind of results, even though some last longer and are more obvious than others. Despite this, few results of work are good enough to give the lasting satisfaction that you would like to have.

Even if the results of your work aren't bad enough to discard, they may have little staying power. You may have to repeat them or move on to something different. The satisfaction that they give you is probably brief at best. So when measured by the standard of per-manence, just as by the standards of motivation, intentions, and quality of execution, the possibility of doing "good works" still seems remote.

Eventual results. The most unpredictable aspect of your work is the far-reaching results of your work that you can't even know. Your actions take on a life of their own, setting in motion forces beyond your control. Your actions eventually spin out a web of re-actions that you can't predict. Even actions that fulfill your good intentions can do damage that you never expected. For example, you may build a building using insulation material that is thought to be harmless, that serves a good purpose, and that is the best quality available at the time you use it. Yet many years later that material is found to have harmful effects as it ages. Even though your intentions in using the material were good, the eventual result was harmful.

Since even your apparently good actions can do damage that you have no way of predicting, you can't be sure of the real good-ness of your works. Their eventual outcome can be bad even though your motives, intentions, and method of execution were good. Some results are beyond your control and your knowledge.

So is there no way you can claim to have done good work? You know that you are called to act as God's partner, and you have tried to do good work, but now your position looks hopeless. The possi-bility of claiming that your actions are good is really beyond your control. The final verdict about your work's goodness is always mixed at best.

You may try to silence the verdict by lowering your standards, but you know this isn't a real solution to the problem. You find that you are headed toward a goal that you can't reach, in a race that you can't drop out of. All the questions have changed. Evidently the goodness of your works can't come from anything that you do.

Maybe I'll try another way

Still, it's hard to give up. The temptation to try to salvage some goodness for your works through your own efforts is strong. People do this in three main ways, all of which are self-defeating.

The most heroic way in which people try to achieve goodness is by *reforming the world*, and this is an admirable way. The world needs our works, and reformers doggedly hang on to that fact. They refuse to surrender the world to the forces of disintegration; however, reformers' efforts never completely succeed. Their visions never encompass the whole.

Reformers can rearrange the furniture in useful ways, but they can't move us into a new house. Our basic human condition can't be changed. Reformers therefore often become bitter or arrogant. They tend to see everyone who questions their proposals as an enemy rather than as a member of the loyal opposition. The results of reformers' works are always ambiguous, so being a reformer doesn't guarantee that your work will be considered good.

Instead of trying to be reformers, many people try a different way that sometimes looks equally heroic: they *renounce the world*. This is not easy either to begin or to continue. It is not a position that a weak person can maintain; you have to be strong and brave to do it. It isn't without effect on the world, either. Renouncing the established value system and using a different one poses a real threat to the existing system – a more serious threat than reform, in fact. People who live according to a different system present the whole society with an option that it can't ignore.

But this kind of threat can't last. If a new system fails to attract followers it will gradually disappear. If it succeeds, the forces it originally opposed will eventually overcome it by joining it. Either way, the new alternative can't radically change the human condition. In the end it will lose the spark that gave it life. So the effect of renunciation is shallow and temporary. Its works have no legitimate claim to goodness.

A few heroic people choose reform or renunciation as a way of trying to salvage some goodness for their works, but most people choose a third way. They simply resign themselves to the way things are.

The *way of resignation* is for the majority who aren't strong enough to oppose the existing system or to leave it. Their position is realistic, because they recognize both their own limitations and the power of the forces that resist radical change. People who choose resignation neither underestimate the enormity of the task nor overestimate their own ability to do the good works necessary for bringing about change. These realists rarely make things worse, even though their failure to act keeps things from becoming better.

Few people follow any one of these three options consistently. Most of us try different ones at different times or try to combine them. But sensitive spirits and hard-nosed realists alike eventually find that if their works are to be good and their lives are to be holy, the goodness and holiness must come from somewhere beyond themselves.

God's grace is your only hope

You can't achieve either goodness or holiness on your own. Only God, whose goodness can transform your works, can give the world to you in a new way. Then your works will be good not only for you but also for your neighbor and for the world at large.

When this happens, "what is restored to us is the same world and not the same world: it is the world as realm of [God]."[2] Then your works will not merely be good works. They will be graceful works, because a power of love beyond your ability to create or achieve will have touched your works as well as your life.

Knowing that only God can make works good brings up another question. If people realize that doing good works is impossible, won't they stop trying, causing the world to suffer? This is a real danger, but the other choice is worse. The world has suffered too much at the hands of people who claim that their works are good in themselves. In any case, those who seriously expect to be able to do good works will finally despair, since they will never be able to convince themselves that their works are good enough.

Isn't there any other option? Theologian Karl Barth mentions

---

2. Yves Congar, *Lay People in the Church* (Westminster, Md.: The Newman Press, 1965), 433.

one: "According to the Old and New Testaments it is an absolutely new and astounding fact that a (person) may be a co-worker with God, . . . and that (one's) works, as an attestation of the work of God, may stand under the promise of being well done and therefore good works."[3] Through God's grace your works can become good. Grace is goodness that you do nothing to earn or deserve. It is God's gift.

God calls you to do certain works, grants you the power to carry them out, and then purifies them so that their consequences serve God's kingdom. They are good, but not because of the motives, intentions, execution, or eventual results of your works. Looking at the works themselves you can have little hope, but from the perspective of God's grace they turn out better than you could ever hope. It is better to speak of graceful works than of good works.

God has entrusted creation to you as partner, and God calls you to serve God and your neighbor. To fulfill this call, Martin Luther said you don't need to change your role in life. You can follow God's call right where you are. You can live as a citizen of the kingdom of God by carrying out your daily responsibilities. What matters most is not relying on your works to get God's approval, but trusting that God will use your works to accomplish God's will. God promises to accept both you and your works.

What God calls you to do is to love your neighbor, and your neighbor is the one for whom your works have value. They can't give your life its meaning, and God doesn't need them for God's own benefit. Your call is *from* God, but it is *for* your neighbor.

For that reason we talk about graceful works—works that are full of God's grace—instead of good works. Your works serve others because of God's grace, not because of your goodness.

The real question: Will you trust God with your works?

Luther knew from his experience that a Christian's works could never be good enough to be of value to the Christian. Luther saw that the Christian's work was done for meeting the needs of others. According to Emil Brunner, "All that Luther cared about was to secure the possession of a *good conscience in one's Calling*, and to do

---

3. Karl Barth, *Church Dogmatics* (Edinburgh: T. & T. Clark, 1958), 4/2:593.

away with the unsatisfactory alternatives: renunciation of the world, or compromise."[4]

The issue is not whether your works are good or whether you can do good works. God's promise makes these questions irrelevant. The real issue is your willingness to entrust your works to God so that they can become graceful works – works full of God's grace.

Throughout Christian history, the church itself has too often focused attention on doing good works rather than acknowledging that the works of our daily lives could be graceful works. Christians too often fail to recognize the way in which God fills everyday work with grace. God wants us to get on with our daily work in the world, to which God calls us as God's partners.

The constant evidence of evil in the world can easily cause Christians to want to retreat into the church and use it as a haven, rather than staying involved with the world. We wonder why God doesn't get rid of evil so that the world can be the kind of kingdom God wants, and we don't want to risk getting out in the midst of all that evil. However, when you see how God's grace operates, you see that God intends not to destroy evil but to restore creation. The crucifixion and resurrection of Jesus Christ show that the future doesn't belong to the power of evil. Because this is true, you can do your work in the world confidently. In Jesus you see not only who you are but also how God's partners are meant to work in God's world.

God doesn't promise that everything will go well, of course. God promises only that all will eventually end well. Working as God's partner you will probably experience opposition and suffering. In spite of this, you can still be sure that your life will not be wasted, that your works serving others will not be lost, and that your work to serve God's kingdom will bear fruit. As you do your grace-filled works of love you still must live from faith, on the basis of hope, but you can be at peace. You can have a new confidence, for you know that your works have a place in God's kingdom.

Sin bravely

The world's prizes and punishments don't have to dominate your life. They are merely paper tigers. The Christian's way of living

---

4. Emil Brunner, *The Divine Imperative* (Philadelphia: Westminster Press, 1957), 206.

in the world – living with little regard for the self and with total regard for the neighbor – is the opposite of what the world expects, and just being commanded to live this way wouldn't work. So when you live on the basis of God's grace you are independent of the world in an important way. Luther called this the Christian's freedom.

> We conclude, therefore, that a Christian lives not in himself, but in Christ and in his neighbor. Otherwise he is not a Christian. He lives in Christ through faith, in his neighbor through love. By faith he is caught up beyond himself into God. By love he descends beneath himself into his neighbor.[5]

Luther didn't claim that we could do this on our own. For that reason he urged Christians to "sin bravely, but more bravely believe." For Luther this meant that we would always need God's grace but that we still had to go ahead and try our best to serve our neighbor. We can do so, Luther observed, because we can trust that "God wills to allow a sinful (person), in all (his or her) actual sinfulness, to work for Him."[6]

This promise of God can make a real difference for both you and your neighbor. You can see this in a story that a layperson told me about his experience trying to help people in need through his work as a public defender when he was a young and idealistic attorney. His motives were mixed. He wanted to help, and he rejected his family's belief that the poor have only themselves to blame for their problems. He was compassionate and understanding, and he did everything he could for the poor, but he became frustrated. None of the poor whom he tried to help showed any evidence of wanting help. Although he waived his fees, the clients wouldn't even show up for meetings with him. He soon found himself being molded into the world's way of thinking about the poor: either they had caused their own problems and didn't deserve help, or someone had to do everything for them in order to help them.

The young lawyer's failure could have led him to give up, but

---

5. Martin Luther, "The Freedom of a Christian," *Luther's Works* (Philadelphia: Muhlenberg Press, 1958), 31:371.
6. Brunner, *The Divine Imperative*, 199.

instead it helped him see more clearly how he could give real help. He saw that his idealism had actually been self-serving. He realized that there was some truth in his parents' belief that trying to help the poor with charity was futile, so he began to treat his poor clients the way he would treat any other client. He charged them a small fee, he made them write the information that he needed for handling their cases, and he set deadlines. Most important, he insisted that the clients meet these requirements. From then on he never lost a client.

What had changed? He had. God had used the poor clients to transform the lawyer so that he could be of real use to them. They served as the means for moving him from merely trying to do good works to being an agent for doing God's grace-filled work. This lawyer certainly wasn't a bad person. He truly wanted to help—to do good. His motives were mixed, but aren't everyone's?

This lawyer's main struggle was with himself. He didn't want to acknowledge that there was any truth in what his parents were telling him, because he could see that there was something wrong with their approach. He thought that if he had good intentions and did all he could, it would work. His problem was not with the poor people; he was the problem for them. The way he originally tried to help them was robbing them of their self-respect and dignity. Instead of meeting their needs he was using them to meet his needs, which didn't help him or the poor people.

The lawyer's crisis was a crisis of faith, although it took him a while to recognize it as such. Until God could transform him, his noble efforts could bear no fruit. Only when he was able to accept God's grace did his works begin to do real good.

God's partners do the work of love in the world

Doing good works means committing yourself to being God's agent in the world and trusting that God's grace will make your work good. As God's partner, you are called by God to engage in works of love. Your purpose is to stand with God and see the world's needs from God's viewpoint. You are to trust that your deeds of love, no matter how imperfectly they may be conceived and carried out, will express God's love for the world. Works done in this spirit carry out God's intention for the world. They touch every dimension of human life and every moment of existence.

Nothing stands outside, beyond, or beneath the caring love that such grace-filled works show. You have God's promise.

Love is patient; love is kind and envies no one. Love is never boastful, nor conceited, nor rude; never selfish, not quick to take offence. Love keeps no score of wrongs; does not gloat over [others'] sins, but delights in the truth. There is nothing love cannot face; there is no limit to its faith, its hope, and its endurance. (1 Corinthians 13:4-7, NEB)

Questions for Reflection

1. Why do you do the work that you do?

2. What standards do you use for measuring the goodness of your work?

3. Is legality an adequate standard for measuring whether an action is right or wrong? If not, what other standards matter?

4. This part of the chapter identifies five standards for measuring good work: motivation, intentions, quality of execution, permanence, and long-range consequences. What do these standards say about your own work?

5. Do you more often choose reform, renunciation, or resignation as a way of trying to ensure that your work has good results?

6. If only God can make your works good, is there any reason to try to do better work?

7. Do you agree that your works cannot benefit God or yourself, but only your neighbor?

8. How might your way of doing your work change if you trusted God to make it good? What new work might you consider doing?

9. Reflect on Stan's statement that "when you live on the basis of God's grace you are independent of the world." If a person were

sure of this, what difference might it make in his or her daily life?

10. How do you feel about the story of the young lawyer who found a better way of helping the poor?

11. What other thoughts or feelings came to you as you read Stan's part of the chapter on work?

Chapter 3

Who Will Guide Me?
Stan: Jesus – the Way to Live in the World

Faith's main concern is not "Does God exist?" Merely believing that God exists offers little help for your daily life. You need more. You need to know what God is like and what God expects of you.

Jesus' question, "Who do you say that I am?" (Luke 9:20, RSV) comes to you followed by another question: "Will you let Jesus be your guide?" Jesus plays a critical role in your life, because he is the one who calls you to be God's partner and shows you what it means to do so. Jesus calls you to follow him. He offers himself to you as a guide for living as God's partner.

Theologian Carl Michalson has correctly said, "There is a place in history to which one may point with the assurance that *There* God is.' That place is Jesus Christ."[1] It's easy to overlook the importance of this claim. To see it, rearrange the words. To say "Jesus is like God" lets you forget that God is hidden and silent; your own efforts can't show you what God is like. Christian faith says instead, "God is like Jesus." In Jesus, God breaks God's silence and comes into view. Jesus becomes the content of the word "God." In Jesus you hear a new word about God that can guide you in your efforts to live as God's partner.

The Christian faith claims that Jesus is God's son, not in spite of the fact that Jesus is a person but precisely *because* he is a person.

---

1. Carl Michalson, *The Hinge of History* (New York: Charles Scribner's Sons, 1959), 140.

As Karl Barth pointed out, "[Jesus] is not a real man in spite of but because of the fact that He is the Son of God and therefore acts as the Saviour."[2] How does God work? What does God want? The answer is always found in the same place: the person Jesus!

Jesus is not some strange kind of being that is different from both God and human beings and is halfway between them. Instead, in the person of Jesus you see God's movement toward you to stimulate your movement toward God. God wants to lessen the isolation, loneliness, and estrangement that keep you from living in love with God, yourself, your neighbor, and the world. God comes to you because you are part of creation that has turned away from God who is a person. You want to be like God, and God chooses to be like you. It is God's humanity, not God's godliness, that stops you in your tracks. God "is no 'cold heavenly power,' nor does [God] 'tread his way over corpses,' but is known as the human God in the crucified Son of Man."[3]

God coming to you in Jesus gives you the freedom to be who you are: God's partner. God frees you from the gods that other people propose, seeking your loyalty and claiming that they can give your life meaning. God frees you from the gods you create in your fantasies, which merely confirm you as you are. God's coming to you in Jesus, however, is not a demand. It is an invitation. God doesn't tell you, "This is what you *must* be!" God says instead, "This is what you *can* be!" So when you encounter Jesus you can say not only "There God is," but also "There I am."

As Barth says, "The subject of the story of Jesus Christ is therefore God Himself, as truly as a man lives and suffers and acts there."[4] The story of Jesus, then, is the story of a new beginning. It tells you that God has chosen not to turn away from creation but rather to turn toward it in the person of Jesus. In Jesus you hear that God is for you. In Jesus you see what God has intended from the beginning. In Jesus you meet the one who comes to guide you as you seek to be who you are: God's partner. The possibility of a new

---

2. Karl Barth, *Church Dogmatics* (Edinburgh: T. & T. Clark, 1960), 3/2:58.
3. Jürgen Moltmann, *The Crucified God* (New York: Harper and Row, 1974), 227.
4. Karl Barth, *Dogmatics in Outline* (New York: Harper and Brothers, 1959), 97.

beginning opens up for you because in Jesus you find the good news: God is there, for you.

In Jesus, God has made ordinary life extraordinary

What is essential in your practice of faith is a person, therefore, and not an idea. An idea asks you to reflect on it and then accept it, but the person Jesus asks a radically different question. Jesus doesn't ask "Do you agree?" He asks instead, "Will you follow?" So the unique nature of Jesus' birth is not the real challenge to your faith. The real scandal of Jesus' birth is its everydayness. A young woman from a small town in an occupied territory gives birth to a son. The scandal is that this young peasant woman gives birth to the person who brings the world a new future! God's new beginning comes in the ordinary event of a birth, and God acting in this ordinary yet unique way changes the meaning of your ordinary everyday life.

This lets you know that God can't be found by escaping everyday life. "Everydayness," says contemporary theologian Elisabeth Schüssler Fiorenza, "can become revelatory."[5] This was the original intention of the claim the early church made about Jesus in the Apostles' Creed: he was "born of the virgin Mary." This statement declared the church's awareness of the human side of God's new beginning. It says that the God who is for you is also with you.

You are not being called to leave the world behind. You are being invited instead to see your ordinary everyday activities as the arena in which God calls you to act out your partnership with God. In Jesus, God identifies with you so that you can take on your human vocation as God's partner in and for the world.

The coming of Jesus restores not only your relationship with God but also your relationship with the human community. Jesus was born of Mary and had a human family. Jesus therefore enlarges your understanding of family by letting you know that your brothers and sisters are those who do the will of God. Ironically, the particularity of Jesus' birth is what makes a new beginning possible for the entire human community. There are no longer any strangers or outsiders when you follow Jesus. Jesus, who like you was born of a

---

5. Elisabeth Schüssler Fiorenza, *In Memory of Her* (New York: Crossroad, 1985), 120.

woman, is the one who invites all human beings to be like him. He invites all to live in community with God and one another.

The circumstances of Jesus' birth show that rank doesn't matter to God. The fact that Jesus was born to a lowly peasant woman reinforces God's call to you to become God's partner. As Barth points out, "In the midst of the old the new humanity begins. This is the miracle of Christmas."[6] The new humanity can begin right in the middle of your daily life that reeks of the old humanity; what God did with Mary, God also wants to do with you. So "conceived by the Holy Spirit" is not a gynecological statement; it is a theological statement, an affirmation of faith. It says that the kind of birth that really matters comes from hearing God's promise that the new can come in the midst of the old. Mary's place in the life of faith is not just as the biological mother of Jesus, but as God's handmaid who was free to say "I am the Lord's servant; may it happen to me as you have said" (Luke 1:38, GNB). The real miracle of Christmas is that your life can have new meaning because the person Jesus is "born of the virgin Mary."

"Nothing human is alien to God. . . . Because it is rooted in the human Jesus, [it] is salvation with a human face."[7] Jesus is like you, and you are to be like Jesus. The coming of Jesus lets you know who you are and who you are called to be. You don't need to look for another guide, for in Jesus "There God is, *with you.*"

The lifestyle of faith

The Apostles' Creed expresses Jesus' identification with you by saying, "He suffered under Pontius Pilate." This statement is not meant as a mere historical account of what happened to Jesus; it is the early church's way of saying that Jesus' lifestyle was marked by suffering. Suffering was not his mission; instead, he suffered because he was faithful to his mission. This lets you know that his ministry included real temptations. At first he asked God, "Let this cup pass from me" (Matthew 26:39, RSV). The suffering was real, and so was Jesus' temptation to avoid it. If Jesus had given in to this temptation it would have "disrupted his relation to God and ruined

---

6. Barth, *Dogmatics in Outline*, 99.
7. Lochman, *The Faith We Confess*, 117.

his messianic vocation."[8] If you overlook this fact, you can't properly appreciate Jesus' suffering.

As a person who really suffered, Jesus stands by you. He comes to help you be God's partner in the midst of the suffering that you experience. His suffering shows his obedience to God; he suffered because he was faithful to what God called him to do. In Jesus, then, you can see that suffering is not a sign of God's punishment or of separation from God. Jesus stands by you when you suffer, whether your suffering comes merely as part of the rain that falls on the just as well as the unjust (Matthew 5:45), or as a result of your obeying your call to be God's partner.

Jesus' suffering came as a result of his mission to restore to the world's daily life your role of being God's partner. What you need to know is that you can handle any suffering that may come as you live for others as God's partner. Jesus shows you that you can endure suffering, and he supports you when you experience it while serving others.

What makes the human Jesus so radical is his freedom to care for others. Carrying out his vocation and meeting the needs of others converge in a unique way in Jesus. His caring leads to his suffering, so when you say that Jesus suffered under Pontius Pilate you describe Jesus' entire life, not just the end of his life. The suffering that is his trademark is the result of his acting for the benefit of others.

"The true Lord is the serving man from Nazareth," Jan Lochman says.[9] The serving man from Nazareth invites you to stand with him and thus to move away from trying to gain meaning for your life by acquiring things. Your wealth, skills, reputation, knowledge, talents, and other worldly possessions are useless for securing your life's meaning. Using your resources for yourself is making the wrong use of them. Jesus shows this in his radical humanness, by giving up everything, even life itself, for others as he stands by God and human beings, and this is the vocation to which he calls you.

This vocation both begins and fulfills God's promise for God's

---

8. Paul Tillich, *Systematic Theology* (Chicago: The University of Chicago Press, 1957), 2:127.
9. Lochman, *The Faith We Confess*, 96.

world. You know that you can pursue such a vocation because
when you look at Jesus you see that "There God is, with you."

Obeying God

At one point in Jesus' life the future of God and of human beings hinged on one person's obedience to God. For Jesus, obeying
God meant being crucified, dead, and buried, and descending into
hell. In obeying God, Jesus was forsaken not only by human beings
but also by God! And yet Jesus obeyed, for God and for you.

The German Christian Jürgen Moltmann has asked an unusual
question: "What does the cross of Jesus mean for God?"[10] In Moltmann's view, God abandons Jesus to the cross in order to be God
for you once more. Your partnership with God is seen most clearly
on the cross: in Jesus, God stands with you and for you. Barth states
it this way: "God himself in the man Jesus does not avoid taking the
place of sinful man."[11] In Jesus, God sees the culmination of the
creation of love and community that God originally intended. The
cross is a unique event for God before it is a saving event for you.
"[Jesus'] cross remains incomparable, his abandonment by God
and man unique, his death unrepeatable."[12] In obeying God, Jesus
shows you that God is for you.

In his human obedience to God, Jesus experiences God's absence. But in his obedience Jesus' work stops being his own and
becomes God's work with the power to save us. "The suffering of
God, universally and in the Christ, is the power which overcomes
creaturely self-destruction by participation and transformation."[13]
Paradoxically, Jesus' obedience becomes a grace-filled work because the God who abandons Jesus also is the abandoned one.

If Jesus himself is abandoned in his radical obedience to God,
then all of your works, no matter how good they may be, will also
fail! And Jesus expresses the same kind of disappointment you feel
when your best efforts fail: after having done the most obedient
human work possible, Jesus cries out, "My God, why have you forsaken me?" (Matthew 27:46, Mark 15:34, NRSV).

"We must not take away from the harshness and depth of suf-

---

10. Moltmann, The Crucified God, 201.
11. Barth, Dogmatics in Outline, 107
12. Küng, On Being a Christian, 575.
13. Tillich, Systematic Theology, 2:176.

fering expressed in [these] words," theologian Günther Bornkamm reminds us, for this is "a suffering inflicted upon the dying not only by men but also by God."[14] Jesus' death shows the depth of God's love for you by showing God's participation in Jesus' suffering and therefore in yours also.

God's work was not to patch things up, to keep you from being inconvenienced or even from suffering, or to right political wrongs. God's work was more radical than that. It was not to make things better but to make things totally different. It was to call you to your real vocation of being God's partner. This could be done only by a God who is there for you.

The cross is not just a temporary inconvenience for Jesus, to be cancelled three days later by the resurrection. The cross shows what being God's partner really means. It is the invitation that sets you free. You are free to cope with the good as well as the bad, with success as well as failure, with life as well as death, and with acceptance as well as rejection. The cross is a sign of hope. Through it, obeying God becomes possible for ordinary people. Jesus makes obedience contagious.

Jan Lochman tells about a large church in the center of Prague. The front of its building bears a Latin inscription that means "Hail, cross—our only hope." Lochman observes that this message has been a reminder of life's meaning as many eras and governments have come and gone. He points out, "What is confessed here is distinctively Christian—the cross as the basis of hope."[15] Because of Jesus' obedience, which is made clearest on the cross, you know that the God who is for you is the same God who is with you as you bear the crosses in your daily life.

Of course you are never put to the test in the way that Jesus was. When your work becomes your cross, it is because in it you try to love the world as God does. You experience God's own pain, wounds, and tears. In such moments, because you know of Jesus' experience you no longer ask, "Where is God?" You find that God is with you, because you can point to the dying Jesus on the cross and say "There is God for me."

---

14. Günther Bornkamm, *Jesus of Nazareth* (New York: Harper and Brothers, 1960), 167.
15. Lochman, *The Faith We Confess*, 138.

The bottom line: victory

"He is risen!" Jesus' followers shouted, affirming that his life of obedience and suffering had not been in vain. The one who is raised from the dead is the same one who announced the kingdom of God, called people to a new future, and invited them to follow him. Jesus still does these same things for you, inviting you to be God's partner.

"He is risen!" is a promise to you. God promises that fear will be replaced by courage, despair by hope, and defeat by victory. Only Jesus has a future, because Jesus is the future. For this reason he can be the source of your future and your hope.

"He is risen!" assures you that in Jesus' future your world and your works will have a place. Barth puts it like this: "God no longer takes [you] seriously as a sinner."[16] The God who declares Jesus blameless does the same for you, your works, and the rest of creation. So when you see the risen Jesus you can say, "There is God, before me."

Faith's claim that God has declared Jesus blameless by raising him from the dead lets you see your daily work in a new light. You now can bear to have your work's results delayed indefinitely. Sometimes you will be baffled, uncertain, or afraid, but in your confusion and weakness you have someone to turn to: Jesus, who goes before you.

Death is the bottom line for all human effort. Whatever you name, create, or accomplish is infected with the cancer of death. No matter how heroic your efforts may be, how diligent your work, or how noble your intentions, the result is always the same: death.

This could make you want to give up! But when you look at the risen Jesus, you have the energy to go back to your daily work with new strength, confidence, and hope. Death has been overcome. Your work becomes God's work, along with God's work becoming your work. Because you know that your redeemer lives you can calmly go about your work. After all, "There God is, going before you."

The coming of Jesus does away with questions about whether it is possible to live as God's partner in the real world. Someone has done it! Jesus has changed the question from "Can it be done?" to

---

16. Barth, *Dogmatics in Outline*, 121.

"Will you do it?" When you look honestly at yourself you know that you have *not* always done the work of God's partner. You have fallen short of your own best hopes as well as God's requirements. You know you have failed. You appreciate kind words that urge you not to be too hard on yourself, but such words can't keep you from feeling bad about the shortcomings of your works. No matter what explanations you offer, the cold hard facts remain: you have not followed Jesus and fully lived as God's partner.

So what good is it for you to know that Jesus has made life as God's partner possible, when you keep failing to live that way? Are you any better off for knowing what Jesus has done? You are, because Jesus gives you a glimpse of another option. Jesus who will be your judge is the same Jesus who died for you, and the Jesus who endured the cross will not change character when he comes to judge. When you look at your deeds you dread the thought of judgment, but when you look at Jesus you find that love casts out fear.

The promise of the risen Jesus is that he is always with you and is always coming to you again. So even when your work stays the same, it is new. It has a new aim: creating the community of God's partners in the world. The trials and temptations will still be there, but they will be different. "Christ experiences death and hell in solitude," Moltmann reminds us; therefore "his followers experience it in his company."[17] Jesus' promised return has an aspect of "already" in addition to "not yet." It is not just a word for tomorrow; it is also a word for today.

Jesus' promise to return calls you to be free for the future. It frees you to see the emptiness of the promises of security that the world dangles before your eyes every day. Jesus' promise gives you the courage to forget what lies behind and press on. You are no longer bound by your fears, because you can see that they have no substance. With Martin Luther you can say confidently, "The body they may kill: God's truth abideth still; His kingdom is forever."[18]

You know that at best your achievements are flawed, but this is no reason to despair or be defensive. You can still be serious about doing things well and helping to make God's future available for the whole world. You know that God "is able to do far more abun-

---

17. Moltmann, *The Crucified God*, 263.
18. "A Mighty Fortress Is Our God," Martin Luther, 1529.

dantly than all that we ask or think" (Ephesians 3:20, RSV). Because
your meager work helps prepare the world for Jesus' return, you do
not lose hope. You know the name of the one who will be your
judge: it is Jesus. You say, "There God is, the one who comes."

With Jesus you can do the unthinkable

Journalist Molly Ivins tells a story that shows what it means to
know that Jesus will be the one who comes as judge. Beulah Mae
Donald was black, old, overweight, poor, and tired. She lived in
Mobile, had seven children, and made her living by cleaning
houses. Her oldest children were grown, and two were college
graduates.

In 1981 Ms. Donald's youngest son, nineteen-year-old Michael, was murdered by members of the Ku Klux Klan. A good boy
who loved sports and music, Michael was a student in a technical
college. He helped his mother at home and worked part-time. For
three years Michael's murderers were free; then the U.S. attorney
cracked the case. Two men were convicted, but others known to
have helped with the lynching were not indicted.

Beulah Mae Donald did what was unthinkable for a black
woman in Mobile: she took on the Klan and sought to prove that it
constantly incited violence against black people. The Klan offered
to settle out of court for $100,000, but Ms. Donald turned it down.

During the trial one of the convicted killers broke down on the
stand, saying everything Ms. Donald had said was true. "I was acting as a Klansman when I done this. And I hope that people learn
from my history. I do hope you decide a judgment against me and
against everyone else involved. Because we are guilty." Turning to
Ms. Donald, he said, "I can't bring your son back. . . . Whatever it
takes . . . if it takes me the rest of my life to pay it, any comfort it
may bring, I hope it will." She answered him quietly: "Son, I forgave
you a long time ago. From the day I found out who y'all was, I
asked God to take care of y'all, and He has. I turned it over to the
Lord."

The jurors were crying, the judge wiped away tears, and the
verdict was $7 million in favor of Beulah Mae Donald. The Klan

---

19. Molly Ivins, *Molly Ivins Can't Say That, Can She?* (New York: Random
House, 1991), 259-260.

didn't have that kind of money, so she was given title to Klan head-quarters. She planned to sell the $113,000 building and use the money to help children.

Molly Ivins' comments on the story capture what it means to let Jesus be your guide:

> [Beulah Mae Donald] is religious, hardworking, wronged but without bitterness. . . . She shows such strength and such cheer in the face of a rather grim life that it's almost awesome. . . . It has been observed that you cannot change an established order with good manners, great charm, or Christian resignation, all traditional virtues of women. . . . It is [her eight] children she sent out to fight the world's injustice. When one of them was victimized by it, then she fought for her child. She not only beat the Klan, she may have broken it.[19]

Beulah Mae Donald died the next year. She had lived as one of God's partners, guided in life by Jesus.

When you point to Jesus you can say, "There God is." Jesus is the center of your faith in God. You also can say, "There I am." You are not boasting; you are merely accepting Jesus' claim on your life. He is your guide.

Faith knows that in becoming like you Jesus opened the way for you to be like him—to fulfill your true vocation as God's partner. When you hear Jesus calling you to follow him, you can say confidently, "There God is! There I am!"

Questions for Reflection

1. How do you picture Jesus? Do you feel that you know Jesus as a person? If so, how have you gotten to know him? How is this similar to or different from the way you get to know other people? If you don't feel that you know Jesus, how might you get to know him? Would you like to?

2. Do you agree that "the real scandal of Jesus' birth is its every-dayness"? How does this compare with your feeling about the unique claims that the Christian faith makes about Jesus?

3. How does "everydayness" reveal Jesus?

4. Is "standing by you" the kind of help you want from Jesus when you are suffering? If not, what would you prefer?

5. How does God's work in Jesus "make things totally different"?

6. What does "bearing your cross" mean to you? Can your "cross" be an unavoidable disaster, like a serious illness? Or does it have to be something you choose to accept? Which was it for Jesus?

7. How would it make a difference in the way you felt about your work if you were sure that its aim was "creating the community of God's partners in the world"?

8. Did Beulah Mae Donald's attack on the Klan succeed because she was a Christian? What if it had failed?

9. What other thoughts or feelings came to you as you read this part of the chapter on Jesus and his role as your guide?

Who Will Guide Me?

Barbara: How Can a 2000-Year-Old Man Help Today?

Can Jesus serve as a guide for my day-to-day life? Sometimes I wonder. I wonder how someone who lived nearly two thousand years ago can make a difference in anyone's life today. Even from people who claim to be Christians, I constantly hear contradictory statements about Jesus. Sometimes it's hard to know what to believe about him.

Jesus' closest companions during his earthly lifetime weren't completely sure who he was and what he was doing; so it's not surprising that we have questions about him now. Even though Jesus was something of an enigma during his years on earth, at least people could see, hear, and touch him then. When that became impossible after his ascension, questions about him increased.

Shortly after Jesus' death the early church had a hard time trying to state exactly who Jesus was and what he had done for human beings. Bitter arguments over shades of meaning in doctrinal statements lasted for centuries and had far-reaching results. In fact, these disagreements caused some splits in the church that are still apparent today. Understanding Jesus and describing him in words has never been easy.

Although they undoubtedly don't intend to do so, Christians sometimes keep other people from getting to know Jesus. Some Christians appear to know all there is to know about him, and they act as if expressing uncertainty or doubt would be horribly sinful. Thus others may avoid asking their real questions and miss discovering that Jesus can be a guide for their lives.

According to the Bible, Jesus didn't think questioning him was the least bit sinful. In fact, he often encouraged people to test his claims. The real problems come only when his followers insist that their particular way of experiencing or describing Jesus is the last word on the subject and must be accepted without question.

Fully human and fully divine

When we consider letting Jesus be our guide, we want to know what he is really like. Is he God, or is he a human being with the kinds of feelings and desires that we have? Early Christians described Jesus by saying that he was both fully human and fully divine, but we can't really conceive of how that could be possible. Logically, no one can be fully anything and at the same time be fully something else if those two characteristics are opposites, as divinity and humanity seem to be.

We can't be too sure that they're opposites, because although we are human, the Bible makes clear that we are made in God's image—that is, divinity is part of us in some way. We usually ignore this, however, so we end up picturing Jesus as some sort of half-and-half creature, or one who somehow alternates between being human and being divine.

If we see divinity and humanity as opposites, we tend to choose the one that we're most comfortable with as our primary way of seeing Jesus. Some people can easily appreciate the human things that Jesus did during his life on earth—his teaching, for example, and the help he gave to suffering people—but they can't accept his divinity. Other Christians see Jesus only as divine and ignore his humanity. After all, divinity seems to be his most important characteristic because it's what seems unique about him. We know plenty of other beings who are human, but we're probably not aware of any others who are divine in the way that Christians believe Jesus is.

Ignoring Jesus' humanity can be the easiest route to take. It lets us think of Jesus as some kind of airy, unreal being and overlook the fact that he was a real human person. And it's more comfortable not to see Jesus as being too much like ourselves: then we don't feel the need to try to be like him or to have to look at the physical, sensual aspects of life. People who ignore Jesus' humanity are horrified at the thought of Jesus being sexually attracted to anyone or doing any of the other physical, earthy things that are part of being human.

This viewpoint leads to thinking that the appetites and functions of our own physical bodies are sinful. We know that only human beings are sinful; God is not. And only humans have physical bodies; God does not. So we combine these two facts and come up with the mistaken idea that being Godlike—sinless—means separating ourselves somehow from the influence of our physical bodies and from the characteristics that we have in common with animals.

Down through the centuries many people have seen the human body as a source of sin. This view appears in the New Testament because it was common in the Greek culture out of which the New Testament emerged. In contrast, the Hebrew culture reflected in the Old Testament considered the physical and spiritual parts of human beings as a unity.

This problem still hasn't been solved, despite the work of theologians, philosophers, anthropologists, psychologists, physicians, and thinkers in various other fields. Evidently no one yet knows exactly what makes human beings different from the other animals, and no one knows exactly how our minds and spirits are related to our physical bodies. Actually, we can't even be sure that matter and spirit are different. Contemporary physicists who examine the nuclei of atoms haven't yet found anything that can be called matter. Some of these scientists suspect that everything is spirit, despite appearances to the contrary. Surprisingly, this is what mystics in several religions have said for centuries.

With all this uncertainty about where to draw the line between humanity and divinity, or between matter and spirit, it's especially hard to know what to think about Jesus. It's no wonder people have such different views of him!

The resurrected Jesus

As if seeing Jesus as both fully divine and fully human were not hard enough, we also have the problem of his resurrection. How can Jesus be alive today? Does he communicate with us in some way now? If so, how? And how can we tell the difference between the living, spiritual Jesus and the Holy Spirit?

In fact, how is the resurrected, spiritual Jesus different from God? Knowing which is which may be easy enough if we only consider Jesus during his earthly life; unlike God, the earthly Jesus had a physical body that was visible and audible and that was born and died just like other human beings did. But when we speak of the resurrected Jesus, who no longer has a physical body and who com-

municates with us only spiritually, it gets harder to understand and
even harder to state in words.

The early church developed the doctrine of the Trinity as an
effort to put some of these things into words. The word "Trinity"
does not appear in the Bible, but by two or three centuries after
Jesus' death the Trinity had become the main way of referring to
what the early Christians understood to be the three ways in which
God was known to human beings. These Christians spoke of God as
the Father; Jesus the Christ, God's son; and the Holy Spirit.

Early Christians developed creeds to clarify their main beliefs
and to get them into a form that could be passed on to new converts.
These creeds have been helpful over the years, but they also have
become stumbling blocks for some contemporary Christians.

Many Christians see the familiar Apostles' Creed, for example,
as a metaphorical statement, while others see it as a literal, historical
account of the life of Jesus, like a summary someone would write to
describe the life of George Washington or any other important person in history. Because of their different ways of understanding the
purpose and meaning of the creeds, these two groups often come
into conflict, with each one sometimes accusing the other of not
even being Christian.

Must we do only what Jesus did?

Similar problems arise when we try to understand the words
that the Bible tells us Jesus used for talking about God and to God.
Jesus evidently called God "Father" most of the time, but does this
mean we must use only this masculine name for God? Many Christians say "Of course!" but others strongly disagree.

The culture in which Jesus spent his earthly life was strongly
patriarchal. Men were the unquestioned leaders in families, governments, and religious groups, and women had almost no legal, social,
or political standing. So masculine words were undoubtedly the
most convincing words for describing a powerful, important being
like God.

However, continuing to use only masculine words for God has
created the mistaken impression that God is like a man and not like
a woman, and that men are more Godlike than women. Even if intel-
lectually we know that this is not true, our constant use of only masculine words for God causes us to act as if it were true. Most

dangerous of all, we act this way without even realizing what we are doing, because the message has been deeply engraved into us at a level that is below our consciousness.

Having been led by God to become aware of this problem, many Christians are now urging the use of more inclusive language for speaking to God and about God. They point out that the exclusive use of male language damages and misleads us. It reinforces a mistaken view of God, and it makes us treat women unjustly as second-class human beings.

In spite of these recent insights about our God-language, many Christians still insist that because Jesus called God "Father" we must do the same. Why should we? After all, Jesus evidently wore a robe-like garment and sandals, but we don't have to copy him in doing that. He spoke Aramaic, but we don't have to. In doing things like these he was merely doing what everyone else in his culture did. It was part of his being fully human—a human person living at a specific time and place in history.

Jesus had to be one sex or the other in order to be human, and he had to call God either "father" or "mother" in order to show us that God was somewhat like a human parent. In first-century Israel, where Jesus lived, "father" undoubtedly got the point across much more effectively than "mother" would have done, because of the relative positions of men and women in the culture of that day. But that doesn't mean that God is literally a father, and it doesn't mean God is more father-like than mother-like, so it doesn't mean we have to limit ourselves to calling God "father."

Christians understand the male role in Jesus' conception to have been played by God, and the female role to have been played by Mary, so this has led us to think of God only as a male parent. However, in many places in the Bible God is pictured as a mother—giving birth, nursing newborn children, nurturing, and doing many other things that either are biologically female functions or were seen as feminine occupations. (For example, see John 3:1-7, Deuteronomy 32:18, Isaiah 42:14 and 66:7-13.) So in terms of God's parent-like relationship to human beings, there seems to be no basis for restricting ourselves to the word "father" when we speak to or about God. The Bible makes clear that God is like a mother as well as like a father. Just as we don't need to copy Jesus' clothing, neither do we need to copy Jesus' use of the word "father." Our task is to copy Jesus' fundamental way of relating to God and to other human beings, not the behavior that was merely part of being a specific person living at the time and place Jesus did.

In the Gospel of John we can find an important clue to the fact that Jesus doesn't want us to be limited to doing just what he did. Shortly before his death Jesus tells his disciples, "Anyone who has faith in me will do what I have been doing. He will do even greater things than these" (John 14:12, NIV).

Are men more like Jesus?

When we try to draw conclusions about God by looking at the human characteristics of Jesus we run into another problem. Jesus came to show us what God is like, and Jesus was a man. Does this mean that men are more God-like, or more Jesus-like, than women?

Some Christians think that it does. Many churches today are embroiled in controversy over the question of whether women should be ordained, because we see clergy as playing the Jesus role in the church. In our communion rites, for example, a priest or pastor serves the communion elements, reenacting the role that Jesus played at his last supper with his disciples before he was crucified. And in all other functions of the church, we tend to see the pastor as filling the role that Jesus filled in the lives of his followers: the shepherd, guide, and healer, and the one who delegated authority to a group of followers to carry on his ministry.

Some people have trouble seeing women in these roles in our churches, and some Christian denominations still refuse to allow women to be ordained. They don't think women belong in the line of succession that began with Jesus' first twelve male disciples. But this viewpoint overlooks the fact that some of Jesus' strongest followers during his earthly life were women. The early church evidently recognized this fact: they called Mary of Magdala "the apostle to the apostles" because of the key role she played in Jesus' life.

The Gospels include plentiful evidence of the major role that women played in Jesus' ministry. And the men in Jesus' inner circle of twelve are often shown as baffled about who he was and what he was intended to do, while the women usually understand fully. Jesus' male followers were often what today's slang would call "clueless," but the women tended to be open to his message and grasp it immediately. The patriarchal culture of Jesus' time and of all the centuries since then has kept us from noticing this important fact about Jesus' followers, but it's right there in the Bible to be found by anyone who looks for it. Evidently Jesus considered women fully qualified—maybe even more qualified than men!—to be his representatives and carry his message to the world. Can we afford to do less?

Words can't contain God

In thinking about Jesus, it's easy to be misled by the words of traditional creeds or even by words in the Bible. It's easy to assume that the English words in our favorite translation of the Bible were dictated by God, but they weren't. They have come to us through many human beings—speakers, hearers, copiers, and translators whose attitudes, beliefs, and personalities have all colored the finished product.

Besides the influence of all these human beings who have contributed to the words we find in our Bible, the problems of translation from one language to another bring even more variety into the Bible's words. Because of differences in languages and cultures, translation can never be exact. There are often several equally "right" ways of translating a given word or phrase, which results in the many versions of the Bible we have today.

The gender of words in different languages adds a twist that is especially important when we try to decide about issues like whether to use masculine words for God. In Hebrew and Greek, the original languages of the Bible, words are either masculine or feminine even though they refer to objects that English-speakers see as having no gender. Consequently, when Hebrew and Greek are translated into English some of the gender-related meaning is lost. We see this, for example, in the fact that the Hebrew word for "spirit" is feminine, yet in English translations of the Bible that word is usually treated as either masculine or neuter.

So we can't say that any particular word or group of words in any one version of the Bible are God's exact words. When we do so, we make the Bible into an idol. We make a human product—the words of writers and translators—into an object of worship. The Bible's words weren't meant to be like art objects, admired for their own sake and preserved like museum pieces. The Bible's words need to be used instead like windows or lenses through which we can see God.

Jesus once warned some of his followers about using Scripture as an end in itself rather than seeing its true intent. They were criti-

cizing him for doing something on the Sabbath day that they considered a violation of one of God's commandments. Jesus told them to
look at him—the one whom the Scriptures spoke about—instead of
assuming that the words of Scripture were God's complete message.
"You diligently study the Scriptures," Jesus said, "because you think
that by them you possess eternal life. These are the Scriptures that
testify about me, yet you refuse to come to me to have life" (John
5:39-40, NIV).

Jesus is God's living Word, and the Bible's words tell us about
God and Jesus. God is infinite, but all human words, including those
that make up the Bible, are finite. God is unlimited, but all human
words are limited. As soon as we put something into words we limit
it, so there's no way we can fully describe God in words. All words
about God are merely finite human efforts to describe a reality that
is infinite and therefore undescribable. Even though the Bible's authors were inspired by God, they were still human, and any human
person's act of receiving God's message and putting it into words
shrinks and distorts that message to some extent. It's unavoidable.

Some people have called the Bible God's autobiography, but it is
actually more like an authorized biography. God inspired certain human beings to write about God and revealed certain insights to
them. But because God's revelation had to be received by humans
and put into human words, the finished product couldn't be a perfect
or complete description of God or of all of God's action in human
history. The Bible shows us God, but it also shows us the writers'
personalities and some of the writers' misunderstandings and limitations. In addition, the Bible only covers part of the story of God's
interaction with human beings. That story is still going on. Through
all the centuries after the last book in the Bible was written, right up
to this minute, God has kept speaking to human beings.

That's why it's important that we have the living Jesus with us
today. He is God's word for us. We can't assume that we have captured God in a package when we've quoted some words from a
creed or even from the Bible. God won't fit into any of our packages,
no matter how beautiful or how large they may be, but often we
mistake the packages for God and worship them instead. If we want
to keep growing in our knowledge of God, as God calls us to do, we
have to risk ripping some old packages open and finding larger
ones. After all, if God could be fully contained in any human words
or concepts, God wouldn't be God.

Jesus turned the job over to us

If we let Jesus be our guide, what will he guide us to do? The Gospels make it clear that Jesus came to earth to show us what God is like, then he left us here to take over the job. "While I am in the world," Jesus told his followers, "I am the light of the world" (John 9:5, NIV). Shortly before his death he explained further. He told them then, "You are going to have the light just a little while longer. . . . Put your trust in the light while you have it, so that you may become [children] of light" (John 12:35-36, NIV). At another time Jesus told his hearers, "You are the light of the world. . . . Let your light shine before [others], that they may see your good deeds and praise your Father in heaven" (Matthew 5:14-16, NIV). So evidently we are supposed to do in today's world what Jesus did in the world of his day. We're supposed to take over where his earthly life left off—to show the world what God is like.

The early church expressed this call by saying that the church is the body of Christ: church members are to do the same kind of things that Jesus' human body did during his earthly lifetime—healing people, feeding them, freeing them from oppression, and enlightening them. Maybe the best description of what Jesus understood to be his assignment from God—his mission—is found in the book of Luke. Somewhat like the inaugural address that a new president makes telling what he or she intends to do during his or her term of office, Jesus made this statement as he began his earthly ministry: "The Spirit of [God] is on me, because [God] has anointed me to preach good news to the poor. [God] has sent me to proclaim freedom for the prisoners and recovery of sight for the blind, to release the oppressed, to proclaim the year of [God's] favor" (Luke 4:18-19, NIV). These evidently are the ministries that God calls us to perform in today's world, following the example that Jesus set for us.

It is possible that the church as Jesus' current earthly body will have to die someday just as Jesus' original earthly body did, to be resurrected in a completely different form that will expand God's ministry in some way that we can't even imagine. This thought may seem shocking, but it's consistent with a lot of what Jesus said. After telling how a seed must die in order to multiply, for example, he pointed out that only the person who hated his or her life in this world would keep it for eternal life (John 12:24-25). At another time he said, "Whoever loses his life for my sake will find it" (Matthew 10:39, NIV).

Of course this doesn't mean that physical life and health are not important. Too often Christians have acted as if the assurance of a life with God after death was all that mattered. They've used this as an excuse for not doing anything to remedy earthly suffering. But this clearly was not what Jesus had in mind. He repeatedly told his followers to go the aid of people who were being mistreated or were suffering for any reason, and his whole earthly life was spent doing so. It's our *own* comfort and survival that he warns us not to make our main goal.

Unfortunately, we tend to hear only the comforting parts of Jesus' message and ignore the disturbing ones. We focus on the sweet baby Jesus of the Christmas story and the soothing Jesus who said "My peace I give you" (John 14:27, NIV). We overlook the Jesus who made radical statements and acted in radical ways—who said things like "I did not come to bring peace, but a sword" (Matthew 10:34, NIV). We like to see Jesus' message as a pain-killer, a sedative, a tranquilizer, a reassurance that what we're doing is okay. We prefer to forget that he directed his harshest words at the religious people— the people who were most confident that they knew all about God, were obeying all of God's rules, and were appointed by God to see that everyone else obeyed the rules.

Jesus guides firmly and compassionately

What kind of guidance can we expect from Jesus? Based on what we read about him in the Bible, we can't expect him to encourage behavior that is less than the best. He rarely told anyone, "You're doing exactly right. Just keep doing what you're doing." Many of us like to imagine Jesus telling us that, but that's not the kind of guidance we find him giving in the Bible. Instead, he shows people their best selves and points out how that differs from their current way of seeing themselves.

Jesus rarely shouted at people or shunned them, however, as we often tend to do when we see people doing what we think is wrong. If we follow him as our guide, we'll be compassionate toward others. The Gospel writers often mention Jesus' compassion toward sinners. He said such things as, "Go and sin no more," but he almost never yelled at the culprits or cut them to ribbons with his words or tried to change them forcibly like some people do who claim to be Jesus' followers today. When I see how some Christians attack people who disagree with them, I can't believe that I'm seeing followers of Jesus.

Jesus evidently didn't even get too concerned over things like false teachers or people who went around misquoting him. One Gospel author shows Jesus merely saying, "Whoever is not against us is for us," when his disciples report that someone is falsely claiming to be one of his followers (Mark 9:40, NIV).

Jesus' fiercest words were directed not at people who broke the rules but at the religious traditionalists who not only insisted on harsh enforcement of rules but also kept adding to them. These religious people's self-righteousness and narrow understanding of God kept them from receiving the messages brought by God's own prophets, including Jesus himself.

We hear a lot about Jesus, and the statements don't all agree. Different people, even if they are all Christians, have widely differing beliefs about him. Evidently this problem already existed during Jesus' earthly lifetime, because he asked his disciples, "Who do the crowds say I am?"

He still asks that question today, and we, like his original followers, report an assortment of things we've heard. But these secondhand reports aren't enough. They weren't then, and they aren't now. Jesus persists. "But what about you?" he asks. "Who do you say I am?" (Luke 9:18-20, NIV).

Jesus made it quite clear that mere words aren't the real answer to this question; our everyday lives are the answers. If we truly believe that Jesus is God's chosen one, we follow him. With his earthly life and resurrected presence as our guide, we try to discern and obey God's will for our own time and place, as Jesus did for his.

Questions for Reflection

1. What questions or doubts do you have about Jesus? Is there anyone with whom you could talk about them? If not, you might want to ask God to lead you to someone.

2. What kinds of things do Christians sometimes do that keep people from asking their real questions?

3. Which aspect of Jesus' nature can you accept most easily—his humanity or his divinity?

4. Do you ever feel aware of the presence of Jesus in your daily life? If so, how do you recognize this presence as Jesus, rather than God the Father or the Holy Spirit?

5. How do you feel about the use of creeds in worship services?

6. How important do you consider Jesus' use of the name "Father" for God to be for Christians today?

7. In the pastoral or priestly role in the church (leading in the communion or eucharistic ritual, for example), can a woman represent Jesus for you as well as a man can? If not, why?

8. Do you find the use of a variety of translations of the Bible helpful or troublesome? How do you feel when you hear or read a familiar passage (like the Twenty-third Psalm or the Lord's Prayer) in an unfamiliar translation?

9. Is the Bible God's last word on the subjects it covers? Or have people who lived in later years received equally important revelations from God? Can more recent insights ever be more important than what the Bible says?

10. How might you "take over where Jesus left off"? Is this what God expects?

11. What responsibility do you think Christians have for seeing that people obey God's rules?

12. How can a person's daily life tell who he or she really believes Jesus is? What does your daily life say about your view of Jesus?

13. What other thoughts or feelings came to you as you read Barbara's comments about Jesus?

Chapter 4

What Resources Do I Have?
Barbara: You Have a Hot Line to God

Several years ago, when relations between the United States and the Soviet Union were especially tense, many people feared that a terrible global war would be started accidentally. Both countries had developed nuclear weapons systems that could be put into operation at a moment's notice, and once the weapons were triggered their operation would be controlled by computers. An all-out war could be underway, government leaders feared, before anyone found that what had triggered it was only a false alarm.

To avoid this kind of disaster, the president of the United States and his counterpart in the Soviet Union got a "hot line"—a special telephone line for their use alone. The hot-line phones traveled with the two leaders wherever they went, so that at the slightest hint of trouble they could instantly consult each other and decide what to do about it.

I often feel the need for this kind of hot line, not to another person but to God, when I'm confronted with a crisis or the need to make a hard decision. Having Jesus as a model and teacher is fine, but Jesus lived in a world very different from mine. I often encounter situations that Jesus doesn't seem to have left any specific instructions about.

I can read the Bible, of course, to find out what Jesus said and did, and then I can try to do something similar, but sometimes my situation doesn't seem much like any that the Bible describes. Then I wish I had God or Jesus available in person to answer my specific questions and give me some concrete advice. This is especially true when a sudden crisis seems to have the potential for triggering a major disaster.

At times like this I discover the aspect of God's nature that the Bible calls the Holy Spirit, the Spirit of God, and the Spirit of Jesus. It's like having God at the other end of a hot line.

The Holy Spirit makes connections

The Holy Spirit is God made apparent to us in a certain way. The Holy Spirit is God present in our midst—God's power within and among us. Like the power that makes a telephone work, the Holy Spirit makes a hot line to God continually available.

God's Spirit communicates, attracts, and makes connections. The Holy Spirit draws us to God and to each other, creating communication, relationship, and community. The Holy Spirit brings the diverse parts of individuals and groups into harmony. The Holy Spirit brings God's messages to our attention, empowers us to act on them, and motivates us to do so. Our human spirits are enlivened when God's Spirit draws them into participation with God and with other human beings.

I'm often startled by what happens when the Holy Spirit goes into action and makes connections between people. I remember one of the first times I realized that God was nudging me toward doing something. I kept feeling the nudge, and finally I dared to say "yes" to God without having the remotest notion of how to do what I understood God was asking me to do. Then I could hardly believe what happened, or how fast it happened.

For several months I had been concerned about a friend who was having a lot of problems. He was an unusually talented person, brimming with energy. I didn't know him well, but we both were active in some of the same community organizations and we occasionally came across each other at social events as well. Each time we got in conversation we seemed to be immediately on each other's wavelength. Even when we came across each other in the midst of a noisy crowd making small talk at a party, we quickly found ourselves discussing some deep question about the meaning of life. This man was one of the few people I knew who had read many of the books I enjoyed most, and we had similar views about being Christians and about the church. Our conversations were always stimulating.

Through other people I learned that this friend's life was coming apart. In fact, he seemed to be tearing it apart himself. He had suddenly quit his job, left his wife and young children, and changed to a church that was very different from the one he had been active in all his life.

I hadn't seen my friend for months, but as I kept hearing this news around town I kept wishing I could talk to him. I didn't really know what I wanted to say, except that I cared and maybe that I understood the kinds of feelings that must be making him want to change his life so drastically. I thought about phoning him, but I was afraid that would be an intrusion. Still, I couldn't get him off my mind.

At that time in my life I walked for exercise early every morning. One morning while I was walking, my friend's situation kept coming to mind. I felt compelled to contact him, but I didn't want to risk being offensive. I decided that the only thing to do was to turn the whole situation over to God—to tell God that I was willing to do something if God really wanted me to, but that I had no idea what to do or how to do it. Summoning my courage, I simply told God that if God wanted me to make contact with this man God would have to deliver him to me, because I couldn't manage it on my own and I wasn't even sure God wanted me to try. (God knew all this without my having to say it, of course, but I had to say it in order to make it clear to myself.) Then I mentally moved on, and surprisingly, my friend didn't enter my mind any more.

That evening my husband and I attended the opening of an art exhibit at a local gallery. It was crowded when we entered. I knew many of the people there, and at first I visited with them as I moved through the room. When the time for seeing the paintings was about to end because the artist was to give a talk, I stopped visiting and started looking at the paintings by myself, with my back to the crowd. Suddenly I felt an arm around my back and heard a familiar voice. "Hello! I haven't seen you in ages!" It was the friend I had prayed about that morning.

I had attended many similar exhibit openings at this gallery, and I didn't remember ever having seen him at one of them before, so I would never have expected to find him there. God evidently had delivered him to me, once I declared my willingness to make contact.

During my earlier conversations that evening, other people had been constantly breaking in and the noise level had been so high that it was impossible to have a real conversation. But now as my friend and I talked, no one interrupted and we had no trouble hearing each other. Even though the crowd was still all around us, we talked as easily as if we had been alone in the room, and we went immediately to the subjects that mattered. It was as if a switch had been turned on, letting electric current make a connection between us.

I didn't have to wonder what to say or how to say it. I didn't even have to ask any questions or bring up the subject I was concerned about. My friend poured out everything to which I had wanted to respond, and I found the right words coming to me just as I needed them. I didn't make any pronouncements about whether I thought what he was doing was right or wrong; I merely let him know that I was still his friend, that I recognized some of the pain he must be feeling, and that I was concerned about what was happening to him. He seemed deeply moved. Then it was time for the program to begin, and we each went our own way.

I have had little contact with him since that night. I know that he hasn't returned to his original family, career, or church, so in that sense nothing I said to him had any effect. But I know that our getting together was important. Our paths merely crossed briefly and then separated again, but they crossed at exactly the right time.

When I see these connections happening I realize that reality includes more than just the physical world that I can see, hear, taste, smell, and touch. My awareness expands, and I realize that reality has dimensions I hadn't previously noticed.

Spirituality is this awareness. It's not a pious, churchy, religious attitude. It's simply an awareness that the obvious physical world around us isn't all there is—that there is more to life than what is visible on the surface.

Spiritual disciplines help us pay attention

Throughout human history people have been finding and using certain practices that have helped them turn their attention away from the busyness of the physical world around them in order to pay closer attention to God and to the less-obvious aspects of reality.

God doesn't want us to *keep* our attention turned away from the world. On the contrary, God calls each of us to get out into the world, to pay attention to it, and to be God's agents in its midst. But in order to find out what God has in mind for us, we have to detach ourselves from the world temporarily at times and renew our conscious communication with God. Thomas Kelly, a Quaker who lived during the first half of this century, states it like this: "[God] plucks the world out of our hearts, loosening the chains of attachment. And [God] hurls the world into our hearts, where we and [God] together carry it in infinitely tender love."[1]

Prayer is the most familiar way of turning our attention to God. In the New Testament you can read about Jesus withdrawing from the crowds in order to pray, and teaching his followers to pray. Ever since New Testament times Christians have recognized the importance of prayer and similar practices that help us focus our attention on God. These spiritual disciplines affect our spirits the way other kinds of disciplines affect other aspects of our lives.

If you consistently practiced playing the piano in a disciplined way, you would gradually become able to play the piano better and to recognize the difference between wrong notes and right ones. Similarly, if you make regular use of spiritual disciplines you become more aware of God and better able to recognize what the Holy Spirit is doing in your life. Ignatius of Loyola called the spiritual disciplines he developed in the sixteenth century "spiritual exercises" because he saw that they do for the spirit what physical exercises do for the body: spiritual exercises strengthen our spirits, making us able to see more clearly what God is calling us to do and whether we are doing it in the best way.

Several spiritual disciplines are specifically mentioned in the Bible, and Christians over the centuries have discovered other useful ones. The Bible tells about various kinds of prayer and meditation. It also tells about fasting as a way of drawing attention away from physical food and focusing attention on the spiritual food that God wants to give us. Also, throughout the Bible you can read about the examination of dreams as a medium through which God often speaks.

Christians have found that regular reading of Scripture or other Christians' writings can serve as a powerful spiritual discipline when we read expecting to be touched by the words and then take time to reflect on what we have read. Keeping a personal journal can also be a valuable spiritual discipline. You can use a private notebook for

---

1. Thomas R. Kelly, *A Testament of Devotion* (New York: Harper and Row, 1941), 47.

recording your reflections after reading Scripture, for recording your dreams and your thoughts about what God might be saying to you through them, and for examining your thoughts and feelings in order to discover what is hindering your response to God's call. Writing your answers to the questions in this book as you read could be a good way to start such a journal if you've never kept one before.

Almost any practice that promotes attentive openness to God and draws your attention away from surrounding distractions can be helpful when rightly used. However, the Bible emphasizes the importance of asking God to guide you when you open yourself to the spiritual world, for you need the God-given ability to recognize what comes from God's Spirit and what does not.

How can you be sure it's the Holy Spirit?

It's not always easy to discern God's Spirit, and sometimes people who claim they are following God's instructions cause great harm. You can't come up with any never-fail rules for recognizing what the Holy Spirit is saying to you, in contrast to what is coming from somewhere else. In general, however, you can see from the Bible and Christian history that the Holy Spirit's messages are life-enhancing, not death-dealing. In addition, they are usually aimed at bringing people into communities and relationships, not at separating people.

Also, God usually guides us by showing us our best self and then showing us how we can move toward becoming that best self, rather than by beating us over the head about what we're doing wrong and making us feel terrible about it. God tries to correct what we're doing wrong by showing us a better way and attracting us to it.

Fortunately God doesn't give up easily, even if we're slow to get the message. God keeps nudging us, calling on the hot line, often sending the same message in a variety of ways, as long as we show the slightest inclination to keep listening. A real call from God usually stays in our awareness for a long time, returning again and again even though we try to ignore it.

When they first heard God's call, even the greatest heroes of the Bible didn't immediately do what God wanted them to do. God appeared to some of them in ways that must have been nearly impossible to ignore, but the people still offered all kinds of objections. They told God they weren't qualified for the job, asked God impudent questions, and often waited for years before finally agreeing to do what God was calling them to do.

Moses, for example, was quite reluctant when God first started trying to get his attention. Moses had murdered a man and had fled to the desert trying to avoid being arrested, and he was working as an obscure shepherd when God called him. Even though God appeared in the spectacular form of a burning bush, Moses couldn't believe that God expected him to confront the Pharaoh of Egypt.

Moses made all sorts of excuses. First he tried to convince God that Pharaoh wouldn't listen to a nobody. When that didn't work he fell back on reminding God what a poor speaker he was. Finally in desperation he said, "O Lord, please send someone else to do it" (Exodus 2:11–4:13). But God wouldn't take "no" for an answer.

God's messages don't always seem as clear as they evidently did to Moses. So in addition to all our other reasons for resisting what God is asking us to do, we resist because we're not sure what God really wants. Of course, if what God wants is something we don't want to do, we can easily use our uncertainty as a smoke screen for covering up our unwillingness.

When you're not sure what God is calling you to do, you can often find Christian friends, counselors, and teachers to help you figure it out. You may do this by going to them in person, by reading what they have written, or by listening to their sermons or teachings. These all can be useful ways to get help. In fact, getting other Christians' views on what you think God is saying to you before you take action is very important. It can keep you from being led astray by thoughts that aren't coming from God.

It's especially important to consult several different Christians who have a variety of viewpoints. If you only hear from people who agree with you, they'll probably just confirm your misunderstandings rather than correcting them and contributing the new insights that you need.

Even consulting other Christians won't necessarily end your uncertainty. Some may claim that God is saying one thing while others claim that God is saying almost the complete opposite, with both groups insisting that they are right. How can you know what to believe? You don't know which group is wrong, but you assume that one must be, since they don't agree.

Maybe neither one is wrong, because God's dealings with human beings are personalized. God's messages seem to be custom-designed for each person. What God needs one person to do may not be what God needs someone else to do, and what is appropriate for one stage in life may not be appropriate for a later time.

The Bible portrays God as being somewhat like a parent, and you know from experience that parents can't deal with all their children in the same way, because children aren't all alike. What works with one child may be the opposite of what works with another, because of differences in their personalities and abilities. I suspect that God deals with different people in different ways for similar reasons. What God says to me may not be exactly what God says to you, because you and I are different and God knows each of us.

Also, what God wants me to do now may be different from what God wanted me to do a few years ago, because I've changed since then. I've grown in my understanding, and I'm confronting some different circumstances now. After all, human parents can't deal with one child the same way throughout that child's life. For example, you wouldn't give the same information to toddlers as to teenagers. If a three-year-old asked where babies came from, you wouldn't answer with all the details you know. You would use simple, familiar words, and you wouldn't try to cover all the moral, social, and psychological implications. But when that child was a teenager he or she would urgently need more information to avoid getting into serious trouble.

Parents make rules for young children that aren't necessary for older ones. It can be very important, for example, to teach a toddler never to step into the street alone, but as she grows she will need to do the very opposite: to cross the street and eventually go much farther alone. Although the underlying objective—to avoid getting hurt by a moving vehicle—doesn't change, the behavior needed for accomplishing that objective is very likely to change as the person grows and circumstances differ.

So if God is like an ideal loving parent, as the Bible says God is, surely God deals with each person differently according to different needs and personalities, and God's messages change as people grow and circumstances change.

How can we be sure what God is saying?

Another reason for the apparent contradictions in what God says to different people and at different times is that we change

God's message in the very act of receiving it. Each person is like a lens through which God's light must pass, and different kinds of lenses do different things to light. Lenses with different thickness and curvature bend light rays differently and thus make the resulting images look different, and certain types of lenses filter out some of the light.

Similarly, God's revelations are affected by the people who receive them. God's message gets distorted, and some parts get filtered out. Our personalities, our past experience, our assumptions, and many other factors color and reshape what God is trying to show us. And we usually see only what we expect to see, overlooking what doesn't fit our expectations.

The dangerous aspect of this process is that we assume that we are like pieces of perfectly clear glass, letting all the light through and revealing everything as it really is. We forget that we are reshaping what God is showing us and that we may fail to see the whole message.

If another person is the lens through which you receive God's light, the problem increases. When you hear someone speak about God, or even when you read what the authors of the Bible have written, you have to remember that God's messages have already been altered by that speaker or those authors even before the message got to you. Then you change it some more in the act of receiving and interpreting it.

If you look through someone else's sunglasses without realizing that they contain prescription lenses, you get a shock. You expect to see things clearly, but instead everything is so distorted or blurry that you can't tell what you are seeing. You notice this problem quickly when you look through someone else's glasses, but when you receive God's message the distortion usually isn't so obvious. It's easy to forget that God's light is being changed by the people it passes through.

The same lens won't work for everyone. Eyeglasses that help me see things clearly may turn everything into a hopeless blur for you, and vice versa. This is also true of the words, people, and events through which we receive God's messages. Words that communicate God's truth quite clearly to me may be meaningless or even misleading to you. A speaker or author who says things in a way that you find wonderfully helpful may turn me off completely. Something that distorts or blurs God for you may be the very lens I've been searching for, showing God clearly to me in a new way.

This diversity causes problems only if one of us claims that the other's lens is completely wrong or useless. As long as we remember that none of us can see all of God, and that what helps one of us may hinder others, there's no problem.

Sometimes you're a lens that someone else looks through to see God, whether or not you intend to be. Who you are and what you say and do can help clarify someone's picture of God. It can also keep someone from seeing God clearly. This is a huge responsibility. You're a teacher and preacher whether you choose to be or not. People get messages from you even when you don't realize you're sending any.

Does this mean you have to be perfect in order to receive God's messages and communicate them to others? No, thank goodness! Although God wants you to be perfectly healthy, obedient, and loving, God can and does use your weaknesses.

Unhealthy mental or physical conditions can keep people from being open to God and responding freely to God's call, so various kinds of therapy can sometimes be helpful for removing such obstacles or lessening their effects. But throughout the Bible and Christian history you can find many persons with major physical and psychological deficiencies, as well as many who have sinned blatantly, who have been outstanding disciples of Christ and spokespersons for God. So you can be sure that effective ministry and discipleship do not require complete physical health, perfect psychological balance, or sinlessness. That's a relief—because if perfection were required then no one would qualify!

Your imperfections can actually serve as doorways through which God and other human beings can enter your life. Seeing your own faults can make you aware of your human weakness and sinfulness and therefore aware of the presence of God's grace in your life. Awareness of your faults can also help you to understand and forgive the faults of other people. Your shortcomings can reassure others that you are approachable, not a remote and superior being who wouldn't be sympathetic to their faults.

Your weaknesses can, therefore, be windows through which you and others can see God, and doors through which God can enter your life, if you let your weaknesses serve these purposes. But if you refuse, your weaknesses become walls that keep you from seeing God clearly and letting God in.

What if nobody answers?

What if you pray diligently, trying to contact God through the hot line, but there seems to be no answer? Why does God sometimes seem silent, especially at the times when you feel the most urgent need for God's help? Does this mean God doesn't care, or that you haven't yet received the Holy Spirit? Not at all.

Throughout the Bible you can find people crying desperately to God and not hearing any answer, and in more recent years many Christians have written about similar experiences. The title of one of the most famous Christian books of all times describes this feeling of being cut off from God—*The Dark Night of the Soul*. It's an experience that at one time or another comes even to the people who are most responsive to God's call.

The feeling of not being able to make contact with God is like feeling the need for more light but not being able to get any. I sometimes feel this way when I drive at night. Especially at highway speeds, I rarely feel that I can see far enough ahead. I sometimes even find myself driving slower and slower, wanting to hold back until I can see farther. Then I suddenly realize what I'm doing, and how pointless it is. After all, the light from my headlights won't move ahead until my car does. I can't expect to see any more of the road until I move into the part that is already lighted.

I think God's guidance works like this. God rarely shows me how to go any farther down life's road until I act on what God has already shown me. It's ridiculous, I realize when I really think about it, for me to expect God to put any more light on my road when I haven't yet made use of the light that God has already given me. It's no wonder God stays silent at those times!

So when there's no answer on God's hot line, I may have to get busy making better use of the guidance God has already given me through the Bible, through the words and actions of other Christians, or in other ways in which God's Spirit communicates. I don't need any more light if I haven't yet used what I already have. I don't need a map of the whole world if I'm not even willing to get my car started and drive to the next town.

Sometimes what keeps us from hearing from God is our mistaken assumption that we already know all there is to know about God. If my heart and mind are closed, new insights from God can't get in. If I'm talking all the time, I won't hear anything God says. If I

won't even admit that I can't see clearly, why should God send me
any more light or any new lenses?

In the Gospel of John you can read about Jesus dealing with this
problem. A man admitted that he was blind, and Jesus healed him
immediately. But some know-it-all bystanders were not so honest,
and Jesus didn't give them much sympathy. "If you were blind," he
told them, "you would not be guilty of sin; but now that you claim
you can see, your guilt remains" (John 9:41, NIV).

When I'm paying attention, when I'm open to new insights, and
when I've dared to take at least a tiny step in the direction in which I
think God is calling me to go, I find that God soon begins sending me
more light, surprising new lenses, and exciting messages over the
hot line.

God gives you what you need

God not only sends instructions about how to travel down life's
road and light for seeing what's ahead. God also gives you the equipment you need, the companions who can guide you and keep you
company, and the food you need for the trip. God calls you to minister to others along your way, and God equips you for that ministry.

Some of the equipment comes in the form of talents and personality traits that you are born with. A unique collection of traits comes
built into your genes. It may include musical talent, or the ability to
use words effectively, or unusual physical strength, or red hair, or
any number of other characteristics.

Among your equipment you also have resources that you get in
the course of your life experiences. You may acquire money, for example, and physical property. You learn how to do some useful
things. You may get power, status, leadership positions, and the opportunity to influence other people. All these resources can be used
for ministries that God wants done, but they also can be used for
other purposes. The crucial question is what you do with your God-
given equipment, whether it is inborn or acquired. God has given
you these resources for a purpose, but you may be using them for
other purposes instead.

In addition to your talents and personality traits, God also gives
you certain abilities that are needed for specific jobs God wants you
to do. The Bible calls them spiritual gifts. They are often closely related to your talents and your acquired skills, but they involve devel-
oping and using those abilities for specific purposes.

For example, someone may have a beautiful singing voice, the ability to learn music easily, and the training to use her voice skillfully. She has a combination of talents, personality traits, and skills gained from education and experience. She has them for life, and she can use them in many different ways—singing in the theater, perhaps, or being a music teacher. But if she also has the ability to communicate God's message through song, strengthening her hearers' awareness of God and their relationship to each other, that is a spiritual gift. It uses her innate abilities and training, but it involves putting them at God's disposal and using them in ways that directly further God's purposes.

The New Testament provides several different lists of spiritual gifts (Romans 12, 1 Corinthians 12, and Ephesians 4), as well as scattered references to others. Spiritual gifts include the ability to teach, to heal, to provide administrative leadership, and to be a prophet—a person who can recognize what God is doing in the world and communicate it to others. But the Bible is clear that these gifts aren't the only ones you can have.

The Bible is also clear that you don't get to choose which gifts you get, that all the gifts are valuable, and that God's Holy Spirit gives them for the good of the world and the church—the community of believers—not just for your own purposes. The Holy Spirit's gifts are the abilities that you need in order to do the particular jobs that God is calling you to do. Spiritual gifts draw people closer to God and to each other.

Spiritual gifts remind me of electrical appliances. Some are huge like dynamos, and others are tiny like microchips. You can easily see the usefulness of some, like electric lights, but you may consider others much less important, like electric toothbrushes. The same gigantic power source, electricity, empowers them all, whether they are huge and necessary or tiny and apparently insignificant. That's something like the way spiritual gifts work. Some are big while others are small. Some are obviously useful while the worth of others is less apparent. The Holy Spirit is the power that makes all of them work, and they are all needed for the community that God's Holy Spirit creates.

In the Bible the apostle Paul says that the ministries that different spiritual gifts make possible are like the different parts of a human body (1 Corinthians 12:12-31). Some body parts are large and obviously useful, like arms and legs, while others are small and don't seem so useful, like toenails or the appendix. Some are clearly visible while others are hidden, but some of the hidden ones, like the heart and liver, are more essential than some of the visible ones.

You may not even know that you have spiritual gifts until you start trying to do what God is calling you to do. Like the light for the road ahead, when you go forward you'll have what you need. When you go where God sends you, you'll find that you can do what needs doing there, even though it may be something that you never knew you could do.

Where does God want me to use these gifts?

Your spiritual gifts can be important evidence for confirming your understanding of what God is calling you to do. If you think God is calling you to be a writer but no one finds your writings readable, you probably need to reexamine your understanding of what God is saying to you! When God calls you to a certain ministry, your efforts will mostly be effective when you do it.

This doesn't mean that it will always be fun or that you'll achieve all the results you want. The work may be hard, even painful, and the results may not be what you hope for, but if God has really called you to do what you're doing, you'll be aware of a certain rightness about it. Finding the place where God wants you to be feels like finding the missing piece of a jigsaw puzzle and seeing it drop into place.

So going where God sends you and putting yourself at God's disposal is vitally important. If you refuse, you can spend years plodding along without feeling like you're doing anything worthwhile. But going where God sends you is scary, too. It may be somewhere you've never been before.

This used to worry me a lot. When I was a teenager I was active in Sunday school and other youth activities at my church, and speakers often urged us to give our lives to what they called "full-time Christian service." To them this obviously meant becoming a church employee. For boys it meant becoming clergymen. (In those days that was called "going into the ministry," as if no one else was supposed to do ministry, and unfortunately that viewpoint is still far too common.) We girls were urged to be directors of Christian education or, for those who were really brave, missionaries to foreign countries. It was clear to us that these jobs represented the ultimate in Christian commitment. Doing anything else, it seemed, was chickening out and refusing to do what God wanted every Christian to do.

I chickened out anyway. I couldn't imagine many things worse than becoming a missionary and being sent to some horrible place like Outer Mongolia. (I don't even know if there really was a country named Outer Mongolia, but it was what I thought of as the most remote and uncivilized place on earth, and the place where missionaries would be sent to.) I knew I wouldn't be willing to go there under any circumstances.

Nearly as unthinkable to me was becoming a director of Christian education or doing any of the other jobs I saw women church employees doing. These women all seemed alike, and to me they were bad news. They wore dark-colored crepe dresses and "sensible shoes"—heavy black lace-up Oxfords with clunky thick heels. They didn't wear makeup, and they wore their hair pulled into buns at the backs of their heads. They were never married.

In my Sunday school and vacation Bible school classes these ever-present women led dreary hymns like "Sweet Hour of Prayer" with closed eyes and facial expressions that evidently were meant to look pious but actually looked pained. They sang in ugly, shrieking voices, swooping from one note to the next. One of them played sticky-sweet piano pieces to create what she called "a worshipful atmosphere." Her favorite was MacDowell's "To a Wild Rose." It may be beautiful, but hearing it makes my flesh crawl to this day because of the unpleasant memories it evokes for me. All these women repeatedly used words like "meaningful" and "holy," and said them with intonations and facial expressions that made me want to run from the room. If this was what being the best possible Christian meant—and I thought that it was—then I knew I wanted no part of it.

I could see that many other church members felt the same way I did, but they sent mixed messages. They talked as if these women and their male counterpart, our pastor, were wonderful, and as if being a clergyman or missionary or director of Christian education was the most admirable thing a Christian could do. But by their own lifestyles, appearance, and behavior most church members clearly said that they really didn't admire these professional church workers very much at all.

These mixed messages left me feeling pulled in opposite directions. I felt that all Christians ought to be willing to do the awful "full-time Christian service" jobs, but I was definitely not willing and I couldn't see that many other people were, either. It didn't make sense to me, but for a long time I kept feeling vaguely guilty about it.

Now I wonder how old those grim women at my childhood church really were. They may not have been as old as I am now! And now I'm having to wear "sensible shoes" a large part of the time because of an inflammation of two tiny bones in one foot. Maybe those women weren't as awful as I remember them!

But I've also changed my view in other, more important ways. Fortunately I've realized that putting one's life at God's disposal doesn't have to mean becoming unattractive or going to Outer Mongolia. It doesn't even have to mean becoming a church employee.

I'm sure that God calls each person to some kind of ministry. For some it is the ordained ministry, as clergy. For others it is a job as a lay employee of the church. But for most of us it is putting ourselves at God's disposal in the everyday world of homes, schools, offices, stores, factories, clinics, and all the other places that keep the world's daily life going.

The Holy Spirit enlivens the church and the world

The Holy Spirit gives people the gifts they need for doing God's work in all sorts of places. Using your gifts for the good of the church—the faith community—doesn't just mean using them within the institutional church. It means being sent into the world in order to be God's agent for change—what Stan calls being God's partner. What is most important is not where you are sent. It is knowing that God wants you to go there, and then going.

God sends you into the situations that need the talents and personality traits you have, not the ones you don't have. This means you're more likely to enjoy doing what God calls you to do than to hate it. Even if God calls you into a situation that you expect to hate, like my Outer Mongolia, God changes your feelings about it. And if you need abilities that go beyond what you're aware of, God furnishes them. When God calls you to do a job, God gives you what you need for doing it, whether it is a new ability or a new attitude.

God needs many kinds of people, and God needs ministers in all kinds of places. God works through women who wear spike heels and women who wear sensible shoes. God works through people who are married and people who aren't. God sends people to remote, primitive places and to sophisticated places in highly civilized countries. God needs ministers everywhere, and they don't all need to be alike.

I believe that God does want us to be attractive—that is, to do what will attract people rather than what repels them. But neither a stylish physical appearance nor a plain one makes the difference. One may serve God's purposes in one setting, while the other may be just what is needed in a different setting. What is important is putting ourselves at God's disposal—reporting for duty and then going where God sends us and using our God-given gifts there. When we do this we are the church, whether we are in a church building or somewhere else, and whether we are clergy or laity.

Just as human spirits enliven human bodies, making live bodies different from dead ones, God's Holy Spirit enlivens the body of Christ—the church—making the difference between death and life. When people open themselves to God's Holy Spirit, when they move forward in the directions in which they understand God to be sending them, and when they put their God-given gifts at God's disposal, exciting things happen. God's work in the world gets done. Blanks get filled in. People are brought together.

God's hot line is always open and the electricity is there. When you lift your receiver by turning your attention to God, you tap into that power. Through the Holy Spirit you make connection with God and with other people, and the church and the world come to life.

Questions for Reflection

1. When do you feel the need for a hot line directly to God?

2. When have you experienced the Holy Spirit making a connection between you and someone else, as Barbara did with the friend she was concerned about? How did you know it was the Holy Spirit?

3. How do you feel about the fact that no recognizable change took place in Barbara's friend's life as a result of her contact with him? Does this mean that her prayer about him was not answered?

4. Have you ever used a regular spiritual discipline? If so, what happened? If you are not using one now, you might want to experiment with one for the next few weeks. If you are using one, ask God if it is still the right one for you, and ask God to help you find a person to advise you about others to try.

5. What do you think God might currently be calling you to do? How do you feel about it?

6. Do you agree with Barbara's explanations for the differences in the messages that different people claim to get from God?

7. What are some of the "lenses" that have helped you see God? Who have been valuable guides and companions for your journey through life? What "food" has God furnished that has nourished you?

8. What spiritual gifts has God given you? If you're not sure, ask someone who knows you well. How are you using them?

9. Barbara tells about her fear of having to be unattractive or go somewhere awful if she responded to God's call. What fears have you had when you considered responding?

10. What other thoughts and feelings came to you as you read Barbara's comments about the work of the Holy Spirit?

What Resources Do I Have?
Stan: You Have Whatever You Need

The Holy Spirit turns Jesus' creative power loose in the world, creating God's partners and empowering them to do Jesus' work in the world. The Spirit brings the kingdom of God into full flower and lets it bear fruit, fulfilling the original promise to God's partners. The Spirit enables you to serve others as God calls you to do.

With the Spirit's encouragement your daily life and work find their part in the divine drama that is constantly being enacted all around you. Whenever you look at yourself in order to try to say who you are, you are seeing the work of the Holy Spirit.

Formation: the work of the Spirit

Only the Holy Spirit can bring life, create community, and establish a peaceful order through your work. If your works are not touched by the Spirit of God, they will be full of death and will leave chaos in their wake.

The Spirit reminds you of your responsibility for caring for the created world as God's partner. The Holy Spirit at work in you encourages you and enables you to do the work of God's partner: creating the communities that love makes possible.

So the Spirit restores your true identity and enables your life to express who you really are: God's partner. The Spirit forms you into the person God knows you can be. The apostle Paul says it this way: "You must be made new in mind and spirit, and put on the new nature of God's creating, which shows itself in the just and devout life called for by the truth" (Ephesians 4:23–24, NEB).

What matters most is not what *you* make out of your life but what the Holy Spirit makes out of it, and the Spirit's goal for you is to form you into a partner of God.

Becoming God's partner is neither easy nor automatic. It happens only through a struggle between the Holy Spirit and the destructive spirits, and your spirit is the battleground where the struggle takes place. The conflict is serious, and the outcome is crucial. Unless you let the Spirit take charge, you remain deformed. In the end, therefore, you find that the real issue is which spirit will control your life: the divine or the demonic. The outcome determines the meaning of your life.

Deformity: the absence of the Spirit

One way in which we try to find meaning for our lives is by becoming part of groups. The group spirit offers meaning to the individual spirit, so groups often try to preserve the status quo. They resist change because staying the same, even in a deformed condition, is more comfortable. Staying with what is familiar and predictable is more comfortable than risking something whose outcome is unpredictable. In addition, past experience with demonic spirits teaches groups to be wary of change, and groups who do not let themselves be led by God have no way of testing the spirits to see whether they are holy or demonic.

In contrast, the community of faith announces that the Holy Spirit protects people who are baptized. The faith community recognizes what a person is up against when he or she lives as God's partner; it knows that demonic spirits will attack, and that God-given discernment is needed for recognizing them. The community of faith, therefore, knows that the Holy Spirit defends both the individual and the Christian community from demonic attacks. It knows, too, that such attacks will come from within the community as well as from outside. The Spirit's defense is essential, not so much to save the community as to empower it to serve God's purposes.

You can see this clearly in the ministry of Jesus. His ministry begins when the Spirit comes and takes up residence in Jesus. It is no accident that the Gospel writers show the Spirit leading Jesus into the wilderness immediately after his baptism (Matthew 3:13–4:11, Mark 1:9–13, Luke 3:21–4:13). As soon as this happens, demonic forces attack the newly baptized Jesus. They recognize the threat that he presents to them, and they know the importance of the Holy Spirit's presence in him. The Holy Spirit knows that Jesus has to confront demonic power before serving in the name of God.

The demonic temptations are not presented in the same order in Matthew and Luke, but the temptations are the same. And they are the same temptations that you must confront when you go to work in the world as God's partner. Each of them represents an area of work whose outcome can't be recognized as all good or all bad.

The first temptation is the ability to turn stones into bread. In a way, this is what we all do when we work: we change something that cannot meet human need into something that can. This kind of work is *practical*.

The next tempting offer is power and wealth, which could be used to correct the world's wrongs. This appeals to the *pragmatist* — the person who wants to do whatever will get the job done.

The third temptation is the ability to risk danger and know that God will not let you be harmed by it. Besides guaranteeing success as the result of your daring loyalty, this ability seems to provide an ideal way to create a better world. It represents the *prophetic* role of being God's agent for change.

These temptations have often been seen as temptations of the flesh — temptations that come from the concrete physical world around us. But they are really temptations of the spirit, and unless you recognize this you can easily underestimate their power and overestimate your own. You can fail to realize that to resist such temptations you need spiritual power; you need the God-given protection of the Holy Spirit.

In the end it gets back to the question of who will control your life. You may want to be the one in control, but thinking that you are is an illusion at best. At worst it is a denial of who you are called to be.

God intends for the Holy Spirit to direct your life. The Spirit's work is to create, guide, empower, and protect you, and you are invited to share in God's work under the Spirit's guidance. God assures you that in your daily life, no matter what your circumstances or your evaluation of them may be, this prayer of the psalmist many centuries ago is appropriate for you to pray: "Create a pure heart in me, O God and put a new and loyal spirit in me. Do not banish me from your presence; do not take your holy spirit away from me.

Give me again the joy that comes from your salvation, and make me willing to obey you" (Psalm 51:10–12, GNB).

Re-formation: awakened by the Spirit

Skeptics are quick to point out that nothing you do as God's partner is lasting. Faith acknowledges that human accomplishments often have a short life, but this doesn't mean that your work has no value. The Holy Spirit reassures you that when you work as God's partner your work is not done in vain. The future that you work for is not one that you create but one that the Spirit promises to give. The work of the Holy Spirit is not just an extension of what was or is; it is the creation of a brand new future.

The Gospels tell about an outbreak of the Spirit at a time that was noted for its absence. They show the Spirit at work with Elizabeth and Zechariah announcing the birth of their son John the Baptist, the forerunner of Jesus (Luke 1:39–80). As the story of Jesus' earthly life goes on, we find the Spirit with Jesus' parents Mary and Joseph, with the shepherds and wisemen who celebrate Jesus' birth, and with Anna and Simeon, devout individuals who recognize the child Jesus as the long-awaited savior sent by God (Luke 2:25–38). Later, after his baptism, Jesus announces the Spirit's presence in his ministry. Then after Jesus' death, beginning at Pentecost (Acts 1:1–2:47), the Spirit does a fruitful new work with people in all places and all walks of life.

You may feel that nothing that the Bible says about the role of the Holy Spirit makes any sense. If so, you're not alone, and you're not ignorant or stupid either! The working of the Spirit is a mystery. In its theological sense a mystery is not merely a problem whose solution hasn't yet been found, like wondering who the murderer is in a mystery novel; it is something that is beyond human ability to understand fully. Just waiting for the solution to become clear won't help. So to be baffled by the working of the Holy Spirit is appropriate; it is recognizing the Spirit's infinite creativity and being rightly amazed.

Part of what is so surprising about the Spirit's activity is that it is going on right now. It isn't just something that happened back in Bible times. In fact, the boldness and power of the people who are experiencing the Spirit's influence today are telltale evidence of the Spirit's work. These people are surprisingly free and powerful in serving God and their neighbors. People who experience the Spirit's work in their lives describe it as being born again, because it is like making a new start on life.

Such an experience has a huge impact on your daily life if you let yourself be open to it. It changes the question "Where can I find God?" to "Will I open myself to the God who is seeking me?" It means that the places where you live and work are holy places, and the time you in which you live is a holy time. What you do is holy work. You can see why the psalmist says, "Where can I go from your spirit? Or where can I flee from your presence?" (Psalm 139:7, NRSV).

Realizing that the Spirit is present for you everywhere and at all times is part of being reclaimed as God's partner. You know that God's gift of the Holy Spirit to you, and the Spirit's gifts to you, are given and received in ordinary times, places, and actions.

Jesus began his ministry in his hometown, reading a text from the book of the prophet Isaiah. "The Spirit of the Lord is upon me," he read, and announced to his listeners and to people for all time to come that liberty for the captives, sight for the blind, and freedom for the oppressed were possible (Luke 4:18). At the end of his earthly ministry Jesus instructed his disciples to "go therefore and make disciples of all nations, baptizing them in the name of the Father and of the Son and of the Holy Spirit" (Matthew 28:19–20, RSV). No part of life is to be outside of the influence of Jesus' followers. The Spirit leads you to announce good news, to release the captives, to free the oppressed, and to bring sight to the blind in the world you live in every day.

Hans Küng has said, "The Christian has to fulfil the will of God in the secular world. He does not need to renounce the good things of the world; but he must never give himself into their power. The Christian can only give himself to God."[1] Only the Spirit can provide the guidance and the power for doing the will of God. It is the Spirit's work.

Conformity: making the world more like God wants it

The Christian life is marked by receptivity. The Spirit promises to enter and bring your spirit into conformity with Jesus' spirit. Also, you receive courage that comes from beyond yourself, a courage

---

1. Hans Küng, *The Church* (New York: Sheed and Ward, 1967), 155.

that is the Spirit's gift. Finally, your life is anticipatory: you "hope for the fulfilling creativity of the divine Spirit."[2]

So God doesn't intend for you to abandon your usual daily activities. Instead, they will be brought into conformity with God's kingdom because you are living as God's partner. The Holy Spirit promises to be with you so you can continue what Jesus began doing. God calls you not to work alone, but rather in the presence of the Holy Spirit and other Christians. Using the gifts and the courage that the Holy Spirit gives you, you can perform your work as God's partner.

Faith makes the astonishing claim that Jesus' followers will do even greater works than Jesus (John 14:12). And over the years since Jesus' death, the community of his followers *have* done more and greater things than he was able to do during his lifetime. Saying this is not belittling what Jesus has done or exaggerating what human beings do: we aren't in a contest to try to out-do Jesus. But our mission of service in the world for others grew out of Jesus' earthly ministry and is an enlargement of it.

The services performed by Jesus' followers show that God's promise to fill our work with grace is actually being carried out. "I will be their God, and they shall be my people," God said many centuries ago through the prophet Jeremiah. "No longer shall they teach one another, or say to each other, 'Know the Lord,' for they shall all know me, from the least of them to the greatest" (Jeremiah 31:33–34, NRSV). This opportunity that God gives equally to everyone is an important characteristic of what the Apostles' Creed calls "the communion of saints"—the community of all the faithful, which reaches through all times and places. In this community all contribute, because God has promised them "I will put my spirit in you and will see to it that you follow my laws and keep all the commands I have given you" (Ezekiel 36:27, GNB).

Performance: using your gifts for service

The Spirit gives you gifts for service, making performance possible. The Spirit's gifts are endless; there is no shortage of them. In the gifted community you do not lack the gifts you need. In fact, you have more than you can use.

---

2. Tillich, *Systematic Theology*, 3:133.

Your gifts are not given for your private use, however; they are not even intended for use only within the community of faith or for its benefit alone. The performance the Spirit inspires is for the world's benefit. Every member of the community of faith is to function like an extrovert when it comes to using his or her gifts. The focus is to be outward, toward the world of other people and the rest of God's creation, not inward.

In this kind of community everyone is valuable. The community needs all of your gifts and every other person's gifts, so that all can perform their God-assigned service in the world. Here's how the Bible describes the distribution of the Spirit's gifts:

This is what I will do in the last days, God says:
I will pour out my Spirit on everyone.
Your sons and daughters will proclaim my message;
your young men will see visions,
and your old men will have dreams.
Yes, even on my servants, both men and women,
I will pour out my Spirit in those days,
and they will proclaim my message.
(Acts 2:17–18, GNB)

You may occasionally hear about Christians who call themselves charismatic because they have received certain spiritual gifts; the word "charismatic" comes from the Greek word *charisma*, which means "gift." It was the word used for the Holy Spirit's gifts in the original version of the New Testament. To call only certain Christian groups or individuals charismatic is misleading, however, because every Christian is charismatic; everyone has a gift.

The community of the Spirit is more interested in the ordinary, everyday gifts than in the sensational gifts. Service ranks higher than miracles, because most of us need each others' ordinary loving deeds more than we need miracles. Every vocation is important, not just certain special ones. God's goal is too large and the world's needs are too great to justify focusing on the unusual; the world needs everyone's performance in every place. That is why God calls you, gives you gifts, expects you to perform, and empowers you to do so.

The purpose of the Spirit's gifts is service. The Greek word for service is *diaconia*, and from this come names like deacons and diaconal ministers, which some Christian church groups use today to refer to people who hold certain jobs or offices within the church. This is a way of acknowledging the fact that God calls all Christians to put their gifts to use daily for the service of others (1 Corinthians 12:4-7).

Transformation: the fruit of the Spirit

The work of transformation that Jesus began will be completed; it will bear fruit. The Bible calls the completed work the fruit of the Spirit. You can trust God to bring about transformation because you have been transformed, and your own transformation enables you to take part in the Spirit's work of transformation – the creation of the inclusive community whose most distinctive mark is love. Love is the Spirit's greatest gift. Love reaches out and includes. It acts to unite what is separated. But it also knows that doing these things costs something. The Spirit that led Jesus to proclaim release to prisoners also led Jesus to his death.

The greatest accomplishment of Jesus' suffering was the creation of a new oneness – a unity that values diversity. And God's creative Spirit is the source of both the unity and the diversity. The apostle Paul talks about this in his letter to the Galatians: "So there is no difference between Jews and Gentiles, between slaves and free [people], between men and women; you are all one in union with Christ Jesus" (Galatians 3:28, GNB). This unity that celebrates diversity is now available to the world, because God's Spirit is at work transforming the world.

When we let God's Spirit do its work, the community's gathering is like a party, and its scattering afterward is joyful. Even suffering doesn't discourage such a community. Suffering merely confirms the community's mission; it serves as evidence that the community is doing what God intends for it to do. This kind of community doesn't have to create special feast days to break the monotony of daily life. Every day becomes a festival, because every day the Spirit is creating the kingdom of God. Life itself becomes a feast.

The world would be shocked by a community like this, wouldn't it? A joyful fellowship that finds life even in the midst of death, victory in apparent defeat, healing in hurt, love in hate, and hope in despair. A community that loves its enemies, keeps only the bare minimum of clothing that it needs and gives away the rest, turns the other cheek when it is attacked, and accepts the people whom the world rejects. Yet these are the marks of the community which the Holy Spirit forms. "The Spirit produces love, joy, peace, patience, kindness, goodness, faithfulness, humility, and self-control. There is no law against such things as these" (Galatians 5:22-23, GNB).

The cost of transformation

In such a community, all people, all gifts, and all work have a place. Every voice is wanted and needed. No one is excluded from the community or from its celebration. Yet such a community is under no illusions. It knows that as its members scatter out into the world as agents of the Holy Spirit they will encounter the spirit of fear that does not believe the Holy Spirit's promise.

Karl Barth, a theologian who had to leave Germany because of his opposition to Hitler, found that confronting Hitler caused many Christians to realize for the first time that it cost something to be a real member of the living community that is led by the Holy Spirit. Their experiences made these German Christians wonder whether being Christian was a good or wise thing to do, for they saw that if they took it seriously it would affect their most important relationships. It might hinder their advancement or even mean the loss of their profession and income. It could even cost their lives.[3]

In the summer of 1988, I was leading a study group in West Berlin. We went to see the Ploetzensee Memorial on a small out-of-the-way street. Upon entering the memorial one sees a wall sixty feet wide and twelve feet high, with this inscription: "The offering of the dictator Hitler in the years 1933-1945." Behind the wall is the restored building where Hitler's opponents were killed. It has two rooms: a waiting room and an execution room. The execution room is empty except for eight hooks anchored in the ceiling, on which prisoners were hanged.

In a single night, September 7-8, 1943, 186 people were hanged in groups of eight, and after that night 117 more people were waiting to be killed. Groups were murdered here twenty-nine times in 1943 and 1944, with husbands and wives denied a last meeting before their deaths.

The people who were hanged came from every walk of life.

---

3. Barth, *Church Dogmatics*, 4/2:663-64.

There were men and women, young and old. There were commu-
nists and conservatives. They came from universities and from the
labor movement. They were believers and nonbelievers. They were
clergy and laypeople. They were military personnel, politicians,
and civilians. Every segment of German society was represented.

Filmmakers recorded the killings for Hitler's viewing, but the
deaths turned out to be such testimonies of courage that the films
were not usable for propaganda. These diverse people were
formed into a community by suffering and courage. They were a
community of deeds, not of words. Their lives stood in the community of the Holy Spirit as their actions stood for wholeness in a time
of brokenness and for health in a time of national sickness.

In a speech on the tenth anniversary of an attempt to over-
throw Hitler, the late president of the Federal Republic of Germany
captured the meaning of what happened at Ploetzensee and at the
other places where Hitler's victims were killed:

> The failure of their undertaking does not rob the symbolic
> character of their sacrifice of any of its dignity....The shame
> into which we Germans were forced by Hitler was washed
> from the sullied name of Germany by their blood. Their legacy
> remains a living force.[4]

God's true partners aren't fuzzy-minded idealists living in a
fairyland. They are tough-thinking realists. The praises they lift to
God are not efforts to deceive themselves. They know all too well
what the costs of becoming God's transforming agents may be. In a
world captive to the deformity of the demonic, the cost of being
God's partner is high.

Although the demonic is present everywhere in the world, its
threats turn out to be empty in the long run, because the Spirit
shows love's power over death. It is a power that does not triumph
over its enemies but invites them to join the victors. It invites the
enemies to join the liberating song that can free them from their
worst fears and open them to God's best promise.

The community of the Spirit sings even in its darkest hours because it knows that its song is the Spirit's song that is heard in Jesus
the Christ.

---

4. Ploetzensee Memorial brochure, 29.

Glory be to the Creator.
Glory be to the Redeemer.
Glory be to the Holy Spirit.
As it was in the beginning, is now and ever shall be, world without end. Amen.

Questions for Reflection

1. Think about a group you belong to, such as your family, your church, the people you work with, or the group of friends you do things with. How do you try to find meaning for your life through belonging to this group? How does the group resist change?

2. How do you feel about not being able to escape from God's Spirit? Tell God exactly how you feel; it's okay to let God know your real feelings, even if you feel angry, scared, or guilty. And you don't have to use any special "religious" words to do so.

3. Which seems more difficult, to act as God's partner among the people who know you best, or in a different setting? Why?

4. Who are the captives, the oppressed, and the blind in your everyday world? How might you help to bring them freedom and sight?

5. Do you find it easier to conform to the world's ways or to the way of Jesus? How might refusing to do what the people around you were doing promote God's work? How might it hinder God's work?

6. What gifts do you think the Holy Spirit has given you? How are you using them? How might you use them more fully?

7. Do you know of any community that seems to be the kind of loving, joyful fellowship described here? If so, what enables it to be this way? If not, why do you think no such community exists? How might you help a group you belong to, to be more like this?

8. If the people who were killed at Ploetzensee were not all believers, how can their experience be an example of the Spirit's work?

9. If untimely or grim death is likely to be the cost of being God's partner, why would anyone choose that route?

10. What other feelings or thoughts came to you as you read this part of the chapter on the Spirit's work?

Chapter 5

Where Will I Serve?
Stan: Out in the World with God

Whether or not you are active in a church, you probably have mixed feelings about the church. You expect one thing from the church, and you find something else. Both friends and foes of the church have high expectations, and the church rarely lives up to them.

Foes are quick to point out the church's shortcomings. Most of their criticism has to do with the church as an institution, and much of it focuses on church members' failure to embody the church's teaching in their lives. In contrast, friends of the church keep thinking they can change it to make it meet their expectations. And in response to criticism, they point out that what the church proclaims is still true in spite of church members' failure to embody that proclamation fully.

At a deeper level, Christians know that even if the church lived up to their expectations it would still fall short of God's. Those can only be met when the kingdom of God comes and the world is what God intends for creation. The church is a human community with a divine mission. The mission is given by God, but it must be fulfilled in the world. As a result, the church will always fall short. Even at its best, the church is only a means and not an end.

The church's God-given mission is much more than getting people to join an organization. The church's goal is to equip people to live in the world as God's partners. Too often this mission is forgotten. Clergy and laity focus their attention instead on the vital signs of the local congregation and the institutional system. Is the budget being met? Is membership increasing? Is attendance growing? These practical concerns occupy most of our time and attention.

When church members talk about the church, its institutional or *gathered* life gets most of the attention. We use institutional standards to define the effectiveness of our clergy, and we measure the ministry of the laity by the amount of time, money, and work laypeople invest in supporting the institution. Looking only at the gathered life of the church turns God's intentions upside-down. It lets us forget that the church's faithfulness to its divine mission can be measured only by what happens when the congregation is *scattered* in the world. When we start with the call to be God's partners we have to use a different set of measurements. Therefore, to appreciate the purpose of the church's gathered times we have to look at what happens when it scatters, because the main ministry of God's partners takes place in the world, not in the church's gatherings.

The church is part of God's plan for saving the world. The church is not a human invention but is instead a gathering of people who accept their call to be God's partners. They come together in order to help each other live as God's partners when they are scattered into the world of everyday life.

Real church work happens in the world

Church work can't be limited to the life of the institutional church. Christians live in a variety of human communities and must be God's partner in each one. In many ways they are no different from anyone else, but the one way in which Christians are different is crucial. In Hans Küng's view, they "are different from their fellows in one vital respect: they *believe*. They declare themselves to be a *fellowship of believers*."[1]

What does it mean for you and other believers to be God's partner out in the world in daily life? You are a sign to the world that God has not given up on the world. God sends you into the world to show that God intends to re-create the human community in the same way that God created the church.

The church points to the Holy Spirit as its creator, and the Holy

---

1.Küng, *The Church*, 30.

Spirit's main work is not to create Christians who are all alike, but to create God's new community that celebrates and makes use of differences. "The first effect of grace, the first work of the Holy Spirit," theologian Richard Norris observes, "is the creation of a society or community."[2] The Holy Spirit creates the church as a demonstration of God's kingdom for the world to see.

As a member of the community of faith you gather with others who are different in order to be sent forth into the world. The activity that most clearly distinguishes the church from other communities is its gathering for worship. When you join with other believers to worship, you gather with a wide variety of people to remember the community's origin. That origin gives the community a unique identity that comes from its use of its members' differences.

Gathered with these diverse people for worship, you explore your greatest need: forgiveness. You confess that you have not been completely faithful at all times and places in your daily life. You hear again God's call that gives you the courage and power necessary for fulfilling the vision of being God's partner. You again receive your assignment from God, to be a sign of hope for the world. Your activity in the world as God's partner shows the world that God does not demand uniformity but gives the world a new kind of unity that makes use of differences.

The sacraments that you share during worship remind you of the unity of God's partners. Augustine, one of the early church's leaders, called a sacrament a "visible sign of an invisible reality." The officially designated sacraments of the church are rituals that help Christians see God and respond to God's call.

One of these sacraments, baptism, is the initiation into the church that identifies each baptized person as a partner. It unites you with others who have the same mission that you do — to serve God's kingdom in the world.

You don't have to be like anyone else in order to qualify for baptism. You don't have to have the same gifts as anyone else, or to serve in the same way. Unity that celebrates diversity is the hallmark of the community of faith. When you gather with the community to celebrate a baptism, you remember that what you have

---

2. Richard A. Norris, *Understanding the Faith of the Church* (New York: The Seabury Press, 1979), 188.

in common with the other members of the community is the mission to use your unique gifts in the world in God's service.

The same thing is true of the Lord's Supper as a community meal and a time of fellowship. The fellowship is with Christ and also with the gathered believers, who know that God calls them to be a sign for the whole world. The sign that they give to the world is God's promise of unity and community.

God calls everyone to serve

God doesn't call all believers to go to the same place or to serve in the same way, but God calls all of them to serve the world in some way, as God's partners. Their worship together leads to their service and witness in the world. Karl Barth describes the effect of worship in this way: "From this centre it can and should spread out into the wider circle of the everyday life of Christians and their individual relationships. Their daily speech and acts and attitudes are ordained to be a wider and transformed worship."[3]

Diversity and unity don't have to be in conflict. Diversity is God's gift for strengthening the community of faith, in both its gathered and its scattered states. The variety of gifts, places, tasks, roles, and responsibilities that the church includes are a sign of God's generosity. The variety can enrich everyone in the community; it doesn't mean the community should be divided.

The unity of the community of faith is not always apparent, but this doesn't mean we need to impose uniformity on the community. Uniformity should never be the goal of the fellowship of believers, either for the life of the community or the life of the world in which the community ministers. Besides, uniformity will never be possible. In their diversity, Christians "can be assured that they fully belong to the church, and through it to the Spiritual Community, and can confidently live in it and work for it."[4]

This kind of unity has far-reaching implications. It means that the Holy Spirit gives you unique gifts to use in places of service that are open only to you. They are blanks that God has left for you to fill, blanks that only you can fill.

Your ministry, therefore, is much more than what you do when you gather with other believers. Most of your ministry is what you

---

3. Barth, *Church Dogmatics*, 4/2:639.

do when you are carrying out the routine obligations of your everyday life. Your unity with other believers comes not from doing the same things they do, but from being involved in the same mission: being God's partner.

The word "apostolic" refers to Jesus' apostles – the original followers of Jesus who had first-hand contact with him and were sent into the world by him to expand his mission. The Christian church has traditionally spoken of "apostolic succession," meaning a process in which each new church leader must be authorized by another officially-recognized leader, continuing the chain that began with Jesus.

Clergy have usually been the only people whom the church has considered to be links in this chain. This implies that laypeople are called to a less important kind of ministry. It also implies that the most important service is done in the gatherings of the community of faith. This clearly is not what God intends. True apostolic service is continuing the ministry of Jesus in the world, so it isn't just what clergy are called to do.

God calls lay women and men to perform apostolic service in the world daily. Words of hope, simple proclamations of God's good news, and deeds of love that show people what God is like and what God intends for the world – all these are expressions of apostolic service. They find their inspiration in Jesus the Christ.

Official status and job assignments given by the institutional church system don't guarantee that the job-holders are performing apostolic service. In fact, "religious" acts done in the gathered community may not be apostolic; simple loving deeds done by community members while they are scattered may be the most authentic form of apostolic service.

Laypeople react differently to the church's tendency to see apostolic service as something that only clergy do. Sometimes it furnishes a welcome release from obligation: if only clergy are responsible for doing apostolic service, we don't have to worry about it. At other times, however, laypeople feel unfairly denied the opportunity to do the apostolic service that they find God calling them to do.

Actually you are not free to choose when you will engage in

---

4. Tillich, *Systematic Theology*, 3:175.

apostolic service. God calls you to serve and chooses the setting and the kind of service for you to do, and God's call applies to both the gathered and scattered aspects of the community of faith.

As a layperson, most of your service will be aimed at promoting the world's good in the settings where you live and work every day. Apostolic service aims at establishing harmony within God's creation and at fostering community among people. God can change human differences from liabilities into assets, and God calls you not only to acknowledge this kind of change in yourself but also to help others experience it. In every setting in which your daily activities take place, you are to live for the benefit of others. As a member of the community that gathers and then scatters in his name, your job is to identify the concrete tasks that God calls you to do.

Your apostolic service is anchored in Jesus Christ, and you are included in his ministry of apostolic service whether you are part of the clergy or laity. No service is left out. Some service may be more public and other service more private. Some people may serve large numbers, and others only a few. Some may serve present needs while others mainly serve the future and go unnoticed in the present. Neither visibility nor numbers give a true measurement of the value of your apostolic service in the world.

The main characteristic of apostolic service is love that reaches out to help and heal. Loving acts that you propose to do, however, will often be called unworkable, unrealistic, and unacceptable. You will not always succeed. But you can still be confident, for you know that the community of God's partners represents the "real world" of God's future.

When the community of faith looks at Jesus, who called it together and instructed its members to "go into all the world," it sees that being faithful to Christ Jesus requires doing apostolic service. It is both a privilege and an obligation, and it lasts for your whole life.

Courageous holiness

As God's partner you know that the acts of worship and service done by the members of the community of faith are not holy in themselves. You know that intentions often exceed actions. You see that bold claims made in the gathered community can easily vanish in the loneliness of the scattered community. You soon find that sin is yours merely because you are human, and that holiness can be yours only as a gift from God. You must simply accept the courage to engage in apostolic service; otherwise you can never be strong enough to live a holy life.

Fortunately, you aren't alone in your sinfulness and weakness. Facing this fact is often hard, however, because all human beings take part in a conspiracy of self-deception. We unknowingly choose what looks good to us, or at least what looks possible, and ignore the call of faith. What passes for truth in the world often hides the truth of faith, and we miss the call to holiness.

The actions of your daily life must be measured by whether or not they are the kind of actions that Christ calls you to take. You have to commit yourself, even though commitment involves risk, uncertainty, and fear, and you will need encouragement to let God's holiness shape your actions.

Your actions will often have to break new ground, and the people who are comfortable in the setting where God calls you to work for change won't encourage you. In fact, they will probably discourage you, if not actively oppose you. Your courage and encouragement, therefore, can come only from the Holy Spirit.

Your decision to act is only the beginning of a long struggle, not the end. The forces that were present to discourage you in the beginning will be nothing compared to the power that will oppose you once you have started into action. You may wonder if you can withstand the opposition that you will meet, some of which will be subtle and some direct. You will realize that your own strength is not adequate. You will find out what Martin Luther meant when he wrote, "Did we in our own strength abide, our striving would be losing."[5]

Luther's words don't mean you can't do what God is calling you to do, because you will have help from outside yourself. You will have the courage and strength that the Holy Spirit provides; without it, you could never do what holiness requires. For this reason, confidence is a mark of the community of faith. For centuries this community has testified to the presence of the Holy Spirit's guidance as its members have gone about their God-given callings in the world. The world may reject the actions of God's partners as they try to obey God's call, but God doesn't abandon them. God

---

5. "A Mighty Fortress Is Our God," by Martin Luther, 1529.

supports them wherever they are scattered throughout the world. Their works are used by God, they serve others, and they have a place in God's plan.

As a member of the community of faith, then, you can be assured that you will be given courage to provide apostolic service in your daily life and work and that what you do will serve the world's future and God's kingdom. Christ who has called you to do his work in the world will send the Holy Spirit to empower, encourage, sustain, and renew you. In spite of all that may go wrong along the way, God's promise will be fulfilled in and for the world. As God's partner, you will be given the courage to endure.

The church's universal mandate

God has given the church a universal mandate, but this doesn't mean the church's destiny is to dominate the world. God doesn't intend for the world to be dominated by any one community. Lines that divide humankind are the result of human sinfulness and finitude. No division formed by these lines deserves your total loyalty. The love that shapes you unites you with God, with all other human beings, and with the whole world.

God's universal mandate for the church implies that the church will have certain characteristics. First, it is to be inclusive. The urge to exclude people comes from human insecurity; the church can't afford to let exclusiveness be the norm for its life. Karl Barth captures the essence of God's call to you to be inclusive in your daily life when he says that God's inclusiveness

> *means that those who are genuinely pious approach the children of the world as such, that those who are genuinely righteous are not ashamed to sit down with the unrighteous as friends, that those who are genuinely wise do not hesitate to seem to be fools among fools, and that those who are genuinely holy are not too good or irreproachable to go down "into hell" in a very secular fashion.* [6]

The second characteristic of the church when it obeys God's universal mandate is openness. This means the church must be vulnerable; it can't stayed closed, trying to protect itself from at-

---

6. Barth, *Church Dogmatics*, 4/3:774.

tack. Its very weakness can be what the world needs to see, because weakness means acknowledging the need for help from God and from human beings. The weak know this, but the strong too often don't.

The church must also be durable. Its members can't be intimidated by the powers that oppose them, either collectively or individually. As a member of the community of faith you can be grateful for the good these powers can do, even as you recognize the harm they can also do. You know that their power will not last, but the church's will. The prophet Isaiah expressed this important truth from God many centuries ago. "Even those who are young grow weak," Isaiah reminded his hearers; "young men can fall exhausted. But those who trust in the Lord for help will find their strength renewed. . . . They will run and not get weary; they will walk and not grow weak" (Isaiah 40:30–31, GNB). When God sends you out into the world, God also meets you there; you are never alone.

A final characteristic of the church as it carries out the universal mandate that God gives it is solidarity with all humankind. The church's mission is not self-preservation but identification with others, supporting them in whatever hardships they face. Jesus sends you to serve others. No place is off-limits for you in your God-given mission, and no person is beyond the concern of the community of faith. As a member of that community you don't gather to get away from others; you scatter to be with others.

God calls the church to become more than it is

As God's partner you are part of a community that is radically universal. It honors all races, languages, classes, ages, cultures, regions, and genders. No one is excluded. When you go into the world as a member of this community, you invade the closed societies around you, carrying God's message and inviting the members of those societies to receive the gifts that outsiders can bring to them. Of course, those closed societies will see your invitation as a threat, not as a welcome gift. But the message must be delivered. Otherwise the world's divisions will kill the world and prevent it from reaching its true destiny.

You may see little evidence of the effectiveness of your efforts, but that is not what matters most. You know the world better than it knows itself, and God calls you to rely on that fact. So for your own sake and the world's, you cannot avoid the universal mandate that God gives you as a part of the church.

The church is built on the hope that God's promise gives. The church must become more than it is. God's call for unity in the church presents a sharp contrast to the disunity we actually see in the church's gatherings. The tragedy of this disunity is that it infects the church's scattered ministry to the world. It often keeps followers of Christ from recognizing that they share a common mission in their daily lives.

Because the community of faith falls far short of what God calls it to be, it can't claim that of itself it has anything to teach the world. Instead, it claims that it is a sign to the world. It can show the world what God has done for the world and will do in the future, not because the church is better than the world but because the church knows God's promise will be carried out. It knows that God will transform both the church and the world.

The church, therefore, is an anticipatory community. In doing its scattered work in the world, the church looks forward with hopeful confidence to the goal that God has set for it. As God's partner, you know what that goal is and you worship the God who sets it. This means that all of your life as God's partner includes true worship; you do not worship anything except God.

Everything else you encounter in life is limited and therefore undeserving of your worship and your complete loyalty. The claims that your family members, friends, co-workers, organizations, and nation make on you are secondary at best.

Worshiping God through your daily life also means that your daily work is holy work, and that all of your life is sacramental. Your visible work serves to reveal the invisible reality of God and God's kingdom. Your way of living today shows what God's promises about tomorrow are like.

In its gathered and scattered life, the church bears witness to God's promise to bring every aspect of life to fulfillment. As a member of the church you testify to the fact that the brokenness you see in yourself, in others, and in the world as a whole will be healed. God promises a new heaven and a new earth, giving your daily life a new hope and a new purpose: in your everyday contacts you are to be a sign of God's promise. The most important feature of your daily work in the world may be your determination to keep working for the good of all people and the whole world.

The Spirit gives you freedom

The Spirit gives you the freedom you need to keep doing this kind of work. The Holy Spirit gives you freedom for others, making you free from what is happening at the present moment. You are free for God's newness, and this freedom must not stay hidden. It is the very essence of your witness, and you express it in your everyday scattered life as a member of the community of faith.

To do this, you can't stay self-centered. Self-centeredness comes from a deep inner uncertainty of your own worth and of the meaning of life. When this uncertainty is uppermost in your thoughts and feelings, you can't forget about yourself for even a minute. But when you have heard something that gives you the strength to forget yourself, give yourself, and put others ahead of yourself, you can move beyond self-centeredness. Then you are free to give the world what it needs. This freedom is at the heart of the visible witness of the community of faith, both gathered and scattered. It is the freedom expressed in your willingness and your ability to serve others.

You can't avoid living in the world as it is. However, you know that your main struggle is not with the world but with what God through Jesus calls you to be and do. The fact that obeying this call is a struggle doesn't mean your faith isn't worth anything. It simply reminds you that your confidence is based on the future that God promises, not on the shortcomings of the church in its present form.

In 1966, I was working in Camden, New Jersey, in an area called North Camden. I was trying to find the leaders of this community of ten thousand people. It had been a middle-class community, and the whites who were once its leaders were now older and in the minority. The rest of the community's population was about equally divided between blacks and Puerto Ricans. Both groups were there because they couldn't afford to live anywhere else. People outside of the community who wanted to help said that no one in it cared what happened to it. People who lived in the suburbs and in other sections of Camden feared North Camden. They saw it as hostile and dangerous.

One of the leaders among the North Camden residents was Martha Williams. She was a middle-aged, white mother who worked in nearby Philadelphia as a restaurant cashier. She was president of a local school PTA and a member of a white Baptist church – a quiet and effective woman whose actions were shaped by her faith. When black families had begun moving into North Camden, Ms. Williams and her family had not moved out as many other white families had done.

When I mentioned Martha Williams's name to some of the leaders of her church, they said that she no longer attended services at the church. Later I learned that she had stopped attending when the church leaders had refused to baptize two black young people who came forward during a worship service. Ms. Williams had felt that her worship would no longer be valid if she stayed in a congregation that followed this kind of policy.

In her work in the community Martha Williams was always the one who could bring together people of all races to focus attention on creating a new future for the whole community. When she finished her term of office as PTA president at the local school, she was elected president of the city-wide PTA. What was most striking about her work in these jobs was not so much what she did during her terms of office as what she made possible for her successors, who were the first black presidents of both the local and the city-wide PTAs.

She didn't accomplish this with force, and it wasn't accompanied by fanfare. She did it with what the Bible calls the innocence of a dove and the wisdom of a serpent (Matthew 10:16). She created the conditions and engineered the process that let change happen in the normal course of events. She preached her sermons through her actions. Her life proclaimed what it meant to be called out of the darkness of the world's fears into the light of God's future (1 Peter 2:9). She knew that God had a claim on her life, and the values that shaped her life grew out of that claim. Then the values that shaped her life reshaped the world wherever she touched it.

When you try to live by God's law of love, as Martha Williams did, you will always get mixed signals about what the world is like and about whether your work is making a difference in the world. You can't depend on visible evidence as a basis for your life. You have to live by faith and hope instead, knowing that the world's current standards are not the final standards for your life. As a sign of God's promise for the world's future you will often be in the minority and you will probably be unpopular.

Nevertheless, you trust that the promise that God has given to the community of faith in Christ through the Holy Spirit will sustain you. That promise enables you to live as God's partner. It assures you that you and others like you who follow God into the world to offer loving service can show the world what God offers.

Questions for Reflection

1. Which approach do you use most often: try to change the church, point out its shortcomings, or say nothing? Which approach do you think is most likely to be effective? Why?

2. If you are active in a church, how might you help your congregation and your denomination focus on equipping their members to live in the world as God's partners, instead of on "the vital signs" of the institution?

3. How important do you consider the church's scattered life, in comparison to its gatherings?

4. What could you do in your everyday life to show the people around you that God hasn't given up on the world?

5. How important do you think diversity is in the church? Do you see diversity strengthening the church or weakening it?

6. What is the difference between unity and uniformity in the church?

7. Do you think of yourself as being called by God to a ministry of apostolic service? What ministry is God calling you to? If you aren't sure, how could you find out?

8. What kind of opposition have you experienced when you tried to follow God's call? Has any of the opposition come as a surprise? What kind of opposition is the hardest for you to resist?

9. Is self-preservation ever a valid goal for the church? For an individual congregation? If so, under what circumstances? If not, does this mean the church should make no effort to resist attacks or to hold on to its members?

10. What closed societies do you feel that God is calling you to invade? With what message?

11. Was stopping her attendance at worship the best thing for Martha Williams to do when she felt her church was not following God's will? If not, what would have been more appropriate?

12. What other thoughts or feelings came to you as you read Stan's comments about the church?

Where Will I Serve?
Barbara: What About the Church?
Does Anybody Need It?

When you've realized that God has a claim on your life and calls you to a ministry as God's partner, what do you do? How do you report for duty?

The first step is to tell God that you're ready and willing. Of course, this won't be news to God. But you still need to tell God. You're doing it for your own benefit, not for God's. Telling God that you are willing to respond to God's call also helps you acknowledge it to yourself, and that's important. It helps you start seeing yourself in a new way. Every time you say that you are God's partner or a minister or whatever you choose to call it, the idea will seem less strange to you. Like doing anything else new, the first time is the hardest, so you need to do it as quickly as possible and then keep going.

I experienced this when I first started writing. Claiming to be a writer seemed horribly presumptuous to me, especially before I succeeded in getting anything published. Even after some of my writing had been published I still had a hard time saying "I am a writer" when anyone asked me "What do you do?" I was so used to thinking of myself as "just" a housewife and "just" a volunteer (which really meant thinking "I don't do anything") that I couldn't imagine claiming that I had a "real" occupation. But the more I've said that I'm a writer, the more sure of it I've become.

Recognizing yourself as a minister works this way, too. You don't have to wait for any special time or go to any special place to tell God that you're willing to accept God's call. God is always available wherever you are, and God is always ready to hear from you. In fact, God is ready long before you are.

You don't need to worry about choosing the right words, because God will understand whatever words you use. You don't even have to use words. The apostle Paul reassures you of that in the book of Romans when he says, "The Spirit also comes to help us, weak as we are. For we do not know how we ought to pray; the Spirit...pleads with God for us in groans that words cannot express. And God, who sees into our hearts, knows what the thought of the Spirit is" (Romans 8:26-27, GNB).

Although sending a wordless prayer to God is fine for God's purposes, for your own you eventually need to put your decision into words and say it out loud to someone. You need to tell at least one other person what you understand God to be calling you to do, and to tell that person that you've decided to answer God's call. When you start reconsidering all your supposed reasons for refusing to do what God is calling you to do, which is bound to happen, you'll need someone to remind you of your reasons for saying "yes" to God and to help you stick with your original decision.

As soon as you acknowledge your willingness to do what God is asking you to do, things will start happening. After all, God has been ready for action for a long time, so when you're ready there's no longer any reason to delay.

When you reach this point of being ready to put your decision into action, it's time to reveal your intentions to a few more people. You need to make contact with a community of people who have made similar decisions and who can help you with yours. Having some other Christians to support you as you go about the ministry to which God has called you will be a big help. This means getting involved with the church.

Other Christians can help you stay in touch with God

You've probably heard people say that they can keep in touch with God on the golf course or out at the lake just as easily as in church. Some people say, in fact, that they feel closer to God when they're not in church. And of course you can get in touch with God at any time and any place, but that's not the point.

The point is that you aren't likely to keep paying attention to God without being in a community of people who will help you recognize what God is doing in your life and in the wider world, and who will encourage you to stay committed to what God is calling you to do. Patricia Wilson, a contemporary author, puts it like this:

> *When I meet people who tell me that they never bother going to church because they can commune with God just as easily on a Sunday morning walk in the woods, I remind them that we do not go to church to commune with God once a week. We can do that anytime. We go to church to meet with our fellow Christians, to share the burdens and joys of our lives, and to encourage one another on the journey ahead of us.[1]*

"All this sounds great in theory," you may be thinking, "but I don't see it happening this way in the churches I know about." Well, a lot of the time I don't either, and that bothers me greatly.

I don't find many church members who seem aware that God is calling them to any mission in the world, either individually or as a group. And I don't find many that appear to care what God is calling their fellow members to do. When I look for support in trying to recognize God's call and respond to it, I often have a hard time finding that support in my church. I often feel unknown, unappreciated, and rejected in the very group where I expect to find the greatest support. That hurts! "Why stay in a group like that?" I wonder.

I wonder about my own gifts, too. Often in my own congregation I don't find any opportunity to use the gifts that I think God has given me. This makes me wonder if I'm mistaken in thinking that I have any spiritual gifts or even any talents. God has given the church the responsibility for confirming its members' spiritual gifts, so if my fellow church members don't recognize any in me I worry that I don't have any. I want to say, "Forget it! I give up! I'm sick of the whole mess, and I'm getting out."

At times like this I think that I must have badly misunderstood God's message, or else that God has called me to do something that God knew wasn't going to work. Either way I end up being mad at God and mad at my fellow church members. I can't see any connec-

---

1. Patricia Wilson, *How Can I Be Over the Hill When I Haven't Seen the Top Yet?: Faithful Reflections on the Middle Years of Life* (Nashville: Upper Room Books, 1989), 88.

tion between what God calls people to do and what actually happens in the church. I start thinking, "Why bother with the church any longer?"

Churches don't look like what God has in mind

When people join a congregation in the denomination I belong to, they promise to support it with their prayers, their presence, their gifts, and their service. But many of the people who have made this promise are absent from most of the church's gatherings. Many give very little of their money, their time, or their talents—the gifts with which they promised to support the church—and they also refuse to give service. Many of them live in expensive houses, drive expensive cars, and go to expensive restaurants, sports events, and concerts, so it's obvious that they're not short of money. They play golf and bridge and travel a lot, so they obviously have plenty of time for what they want to do. Some of them accept big jobs in community organizations and do them well, so they obviously have plenty of ability. But they're not willing to give money, time, or talent to the church. I find this terribly discouraging.

Something else I find discouraging is that sometimes it looks as if what succeeds in churches is the opposite of what God wants Christians to do. The groups and activities that attract the most people don't seem anything like what God calls the church to do. It makes me wonder, "Isn't God in charge? If God is in charge, why doesn't anyone seem to be following God's instructions? And why doesn't following them bring success?"

Then I think about the Old Testament prophet Jeremiah. Following God's instructions made him just about as unpopular as a person can be, and as unsuccessful by the world's standards. He must have been obnoxious to have around, because he kept telling everyone how sinful they were. He bravely delivered God's message to his fellow citizens when they didn't appreciate it at all. They threw Jeremiah into a cistern full of mud, imprisoned him in a dungeon, and mistreated him in lots of other ways. His ministry bore no recognizable fruit until many years later, when he was no longer around to see it.

By the world's standards Jeremiah was a failure. He was part of a tiny minority. Most people around him thought he was badly mistaken in his interpretation of what was happening in their society, and they refused to heed what he was saying. But Jeremiah's message was from God. It was no mistake. And a minority that is on God's side, no matter how small that minority may be, eventually turns out to be more powerful than any majority.

Throughout human history many people who have tried to do God's will have become discouraged and angry about not being able to see any results from their efforts. In the book of Isaiah you can read about this happening to the people of Israel, whom God had chosen to be God's servant. They were in the role that was later filled by Jesus and then was assigned to the church to continue after Jesus' death.

The Israelites weren't always happy about the results they saw. The prophet Isaiah reports a conversation between God and Israel that shows how disappointed they were. God says, "You are my servant, Israel, in whom I will display my splendor." But Israel complains, "I have labored to no purpose; I have spent my strength in vain and for nothing." Then Israel remembers that God is in charge, so they back off a little. "Yet what is due me is in the Lord's hand," they remind themselves, "and my reward is with my God." God confirms this, reassuring them that their efforts are not in vain. "In the time of my favor I will answer you," God promises, not only to those ancient people but also to today's church, "and in the day of salvation I will help you; I will keep you and will make you to be a covenant for the people" (Isaiah 49:3-4, 8, NIV).

Knowing about people like Jeremiah and the ancient Israelites, as well as Christians in later centuries who had similar experiences, keeps me from despairing about the church and about my own efforts to respond to God's call. What seems to be failure and rejection when measured by human standards often turns out to be success by God's standards, and those are the standards that finally count.

There are bright spots in the church that keep me from despairing, too. I've gradually come across many other church members who know that God calls them to a ministry and who are diligently working at it. They're out there; I just had to look for them. Some of them are close to home, but I didn't recognize them at first because their ministries didn't happen to be the kind I felt called to. Others are farther away, requiring some effort to find each other and stay in touch, but I've found that staying in touch is worth whatever it takes.

The church doesn't seem any different from the world

Active church members may feel angry about not seeing their efforts succeed and about not being supported by other church members, but what bothers outsiders is more likely to be something different. They get turned off by not being able to see any difference between the behavior of churchgoers and the behavior of non-churchgoers.

Church members get drunk sometimes, and some become addicted to drugs. Some commit adultery. Some treat people unkindly. Some are greedy and stingy. Some are narrow and bigoted. In these and many other ways, church members seem just about like nonmembers. In fact, it's easy to find nonmembers who are more generous, loving, and kind than some church members.

This is true on the institutional as well as individual level. You probably know plenty of organizations that do outstanding service for humankind. Whether it's Rotary International, Lions, Boy and Girl Scouts, the Junior League, or a local shelter for the homeless, you can easily think of local and worldwide groups that do many of the very same kinds of things the Bible tells Christians to do.

Sometimes community-service organizations do these things better than churches. Some people say they have found more help in twelve-step groups like Alcoholics Anonymous than they have found in any church. Some even claim that more understanding and support are available at the typical bar than at the typical church.

What does this say about the church? Perhaps you could follow God's call without participating in the institutional church. Are church members being dishonest by claiming to be God's followers when they really aren't any different from anyone else? Maybe nonmembers are actually the most admirable, because they're not making any such claims.

If church members are just as sinful as nonmembers, and if they don't do any more good works than nonmembers, why be a member? Do church members get some kind of reward that no one else gets? If so, it certainly isn't obvious, because being a church member doesn't keep you from suffering. Church members get cancer and die in automobile wrecks and have their homes demolished by earthquakes, just as nonmembers do. Church members' children drop out of school, and their elderly parents get Alzheimer's disease, just as the children and parents of nonmembers do. Church members lose their jobs, and their marriages fall apart. Life for church members isn't all comfort and enjoyment and success, any more than it is for nonmembers. So where's the reward? Escape from suffering certainly isn't it.

The church is aware of its target

If church members get no recognizable reward such as being able to escape suffering, and if they have no greater virtue and do no more good works than anyone else, how is the church any different from the world? Maybe the main difference between the church and the world is in the awareness of members and nonmembers. The church is the community of people who have become aware that God exists, that nothing else is worthy of their ultimate loyalty, and that God has a claim on their lives.

The church is like a group of people who are shooting arrows at a target. Some people will hit the target and some won't, but even those who miss know that the target exists. They have at least a vague awareness that the target is what they're supposed to hit. In contrast, other archers may be shooting arrows in the same area, but they're not aware of the target. Some of their arrows may hit it, but only by accident. Both groups will hit the target at times, and both will fail at times. But the people who see the target, aim at it, and try to improve their shooting technique are likely to hit the target more often than the people who shoot at random.

The church's target is its ministry of love to the world. God calls the church to show the world that God is love, by acting lovingly in everyday life in the world. When you become part of the church, you acknowledge that you have become aware of God, who is love, and that you have made yourself and your resources available for God to use in the ministry of love.

Your awareness of God may be only a faint glimpse, but it's a start. Your commitment may be tentative and hesitant, and it may often waver, but it's a first step in the right direction, and that's worth a lot. You may put only a tiny part of yourself at God's disposal, but a tiny part is better than none.

By becoming part of the church you don't join a perfect group, but you join people who have at least recognized the target. You ally yourself with a community in which, despite the inevitable frustrations and discouragements that come from being human, you can carry out your ministry more effectively than you ever could working alone.

The church is like a window

God calls the church to be like a window. People outside the church need to be able to look through it and see God. When they look at church members they need to see love in action. They need to see people demonstrating forgiveness, justice, and healing. At the same time, people inside the church need to look out and see the world. God is out there working, and God keeps calling us to come out and help.

Unfortunately the church is not always transparent enough for these things to happen. Too often it is like stained-glass: it may have beautiful features, but if the world can't see God through it and church members can't see the world, the church isn't serving the purpose that God created it to serve.

When church members wall themselves off from the world they aren't doing what God calls them to do. When we stay safely inside the church rather than going out into the world where God is, it's no wonder that our efforts bear so little fruit. To outsiders we seem to be merely gloating over our piety (which obviously isn't all that pious) and enjoying secrets that we don't want anyone else to know. It shouldn't surprise us when people aren't clamoring to get in.

God calls us to go out and meet nonmembers on their own ground, but we're not good about doing that. We more often expect them to come to us. Yet even when they do come to us we do a lot that keeps them feeling like outsiders. For one thing, we use words that aren't used anywhere else; they're like a secret language that a newcomer has to learn before he or she can take part in our worship services or even our conversations. We use symbols and rituals known only to insiders, and we rarely explain what we are doing. We often don't even label the entrances to our buildings; we make newcomers have to hunt for the place to get in. It's as if we've built a wall around the church, trying to keep people out. Even within the church we keep walls between insiders and outsiders. Clergy often treat laypeople like outsiders, and laypeople who have leadership roles do the same to those who aren't part of the inner circle.

This problem sadly resembles one that women have recently become aware of in their relationships with men. It's the same old dominance-subservience pattern showing up in one more place. Women who entered the inner circles of corporate management in recent years for the first time found that even though their jobs entitled them to take part in the company's decision-making, much of that decision-making was taking place where women couldn't participate. The real decisions, women found, were being made outside the office, in places like men's restrooms and men's service clubs. By the time there was an official meeting that included the women, the pertinent information had already been communicated and the decisions had in effect already been made.

This happens far too often between clergy and laity in the church. Lay volunteers supposedly have decision-making roles in church government, but the real decisions are rarely made in the official meetings that laypeople can be part of. Instead, the decisions are made at clergy get-togethers or when church staff members talk in the church office in the course of doing their daily work. Those are the most convenient and comfortable times for clergy and other church staff. In addition, the need for maintaining professional confidentiality gives them a convenient excuse for not sharing pertinent information with non-staff members. As a result, there's often a wide gulf between people whom God intends to be colleagues in the church, and people who should have a voice in the church don't really have one.

God calls the church to be open and inviting rather than closed and forbidding. God wants church members not only to invite outsiders in and make them feel at home, but also to go out to them in the world where they are. We Christians can't afford to stay inside our walls guarding our turf and clinging to our traditions.

To use the gift you have to tear the wrapping

Sometimes we treat our tradition like a beautiful container in which we have received a gift. It reminds me of the way I feel about Christmas presents. I love to wrap pretty packages and to receive beautifully wrapped gifts and then to enjoy looking at them under the tree as Christmas approaches. On Christmas morning I almost hate to open them. It seems a pity to mess up the beautiful wrappings that I've been enjoying.

Often I try to save the wrapping so that I can use it again another Christmas, because it is so pretty and so much effort went into its creation. But this method never works very well because next year's gifts are always different sizes and shapes from this year's. I always salvage some decorations from each year's packages anyway—a glittery angel from one, a poinsettia bloom from another, and an especially pretty bow from another. Sometimes I can reuse the paper from a large package by trimming away the torn places and using the paper to wrap something smaller. But I can't use the old wrapping unchanged, because I need to wrap different contents.

We have the same problem in the church, but it's not as easy to recognize there. The church's wrappings include hymns that we've sung for years. They include the words in which we've most often said prayers and creeds and heard favorite Bible verses. Our wrappings include methods of running the church organization, and ideas about who should do which jobs in the church. Like the wrappings on Christmas gifts, we love looking at familiar aspects of the church and enjoying their beauty, and we feel secure in having everything wrapped up so well.

As time goes on, however, life changes. New circumstances that don't fit the old packages appear. People get new insights from God about what God is like. Those who recognize the meaning of the new circumstances and the new God-given insights propose new containers and new wrappings. New hymns and rituals appear, and words are changed in old favorites. A new pastor comes to our church, and he or she doesn't do things the way the former pastor did.

Our personal lives change, too. Disasters strike that none of our old wrappings will cover. We feel lost and scared. We're afraid that if we discard any of the old packages we'll be left with nothing. If we rip them open we might find them empty, and that seems unbearable. So even if we suspect that they're no longer adequate, we often try to cling more firmly to them and to keep everyone else from tearing into them. We keep trying to use the old wrappings and to avoid recognizing that they don't cover the present situation. And we attack the people who are advocating change.

We end up thinking that our fellow church members are un-Christian, that the church has become faithless or is irrelevant, or even that God is irrelevant. But the real problem may be that our understanding has not grown when it needed to. We may have been worshiping wrappings and containers instead of the uncontainable God they were designed to contain. If so, when changes come, we suddenly find ourselves in trouble. Ironically, many of our present church wrappings were created by Christians who dared to discard wrappings that had become inadequate and to develop more effective ones, but we're not willing to be equally daring now.

The United Methodist Church, of which I'm a member, came into existence only because John Wesley, a clergyman in the eighteenth-century Church of England, made drastic changes from the religious practices that were customary in his church. Trying to revitalize worship and reach contemporary people, Wesley preached in factories and in town squares instead of in church buildings. He and his brother Charles wrote new hymns, often using the tunes of popular songs—even pub songs. But we Methodists now tend to consider Wesley's songs and methods sacred. We're not willing to change any of them even if they're no longer effective in today's world. We try to preserve all of Wesley's creations rather than looking for equally creative answers to today's needs.

Tradition can be a way of avoiding God

The King James Version of the Bible also came into existence because an innovative person saw a need and dared to change the old familiar ways in order to meet it. King James I of England saw that a new translation of the Bible was needed so that people could read the Bible for themselves and understand it. He assembled a group of scholars who produced a translation in the contemporary English of their day.

Those words that were everyday language in 1611 are outmoded now and many of their meanings have changed. But many Christians still insist on using those words, not only for reading the Bible but also for praying and for talking about their beliefs. They aren't willing to take the kind of bold step that King James did. They worship his product instead. When we use outmoded words in church we give people the mistaken impression that they have to master a special language in order to speak to God, to be Christians, and to take part in worship services. This is very misleading because the Bible was originally written in the ordinary language that people used for talking to one another. The psalmists, for example, didn't use any special "holy" words for speaking to God. In the original language of the Psalms, the authors address God with the words that people of that day used for speaking to family members and close friends. And when the King James translation was made, words like "thee" and "thou" and "wouldst" and "leadeth" were household words. Shakespeare, a contemporary of King James, used the same language in his plays. It was neither holy nor poetic language—it was everyday English. But now it is not, and using this outdated language now conceals something important; it keeps us from remembering that we can be ourselves when we talk to God.

Seventeenth-century words don't communicate God's message effectively to twentieth-century men and women, yet many Christians hang on to those words as if they had come straight from Jesus' mouth. Like refusing to admit that Jesus was human, refusing to speak to or about God in today's language can be dangerous. It lets us keep God at a distance, and it keeps our faith from having any relationship to the real world of contemporary human beings. Tradition used in this way can be deadly.

Jesus often spoke about this kind of harmful use of tradition. He saw that people often used tradition as a way of avoiding what God was really asking them to do. When some traditionalists were criticizing Jesus' disciples for breaking the accepted rules about ritual handwashing, Jesus said, "You abandon the commandment of God and hold to human tradition....You have a fine way of rejecting the commandment of God in order to keep your tradition!" (Mark 7:8-9, NRSV).

Tradition is an important part of life. Even for non-church members, Christian traditions are an important part of our culture. But it is all too easy to assume that those traditions are the church, and that they can't be changed without destroying the church or breaking God's rules. We fail to notice that the traditions were developed by human beings. They include human error, so they can never be perfect expressions of God's will.

Religious traditions are like beloved parents. They have made large and valuable contributions to who we are, and they deserve our lifelong loyalty and respect. But we can't afford to let them keep us from becoming the unique mature individuals we're meant to be.

We get many of our beliefs, habits, and personality traits from our parents. They serve as valuable models who teach us how to be adults and how to live in the wider world of human society. But we aren't intended to become carbon copies of our parents. Becoming adult means receiving our parents' contributions but evaluating them as we grow, and then making our own decisions about which ones to keep and which to change or reject. If we merely copy our parents, we remain children forever, no matter how old we may be chronologically.

Like parents, religious traditions and past leaders of the church have made valuable contributions to who we are as individuals, as churches, and as a society. However, if we only do what Christians did in the past we never grow. We stay immature in our faith, and as a church we can't minister effectively to today's world.

Tradition can be a valuable guide for shaping your understanding of God and your response to God's call, but it can also keep you from growing. It can even keep you from following God. Continuing to do things the way you've always done them is like staying in bed. It is easy and comfortable but it can paralyze you. You need bed rest at times, but too much of it can be deadly. Even after serious illness or surgery your doctor insists that you get up and into motion soon.

Just as he once told a paralyzed person to take up his bed and walk (Matthew 9:2-8, Mark 2:3-12, Luke 5:18-26), Jesus the great physician tells you and me to keep our lives in motion. That includes our life together as the church. If we stay rigid and motionless, we can't move forward on the roads where God is calling us to go.

Jesus' disciples who were with him at his transfiguration—a spectacular display of God's presence—wanted to stay put, just as we often do. They wanted to build something permanent on the mountaintop where they had experienced God's presence in such an exciting way, but God told them not to do that. God told them to listen to Jesus instead. Then Jesus led them down from the mountain and back into the everyday world (Matthew 17:1-9, Mark 9:2-9). He knew it was important for them to keep moving rather than trying to preserve the past.

God constantly tells us, too, not to try to build anything permanent at the hallowed places where we have found God in the past. God urges us to remember such things but to use them as windows for seeing new territory into which God wants to lead us now. We can't afford to let them be like stained-glass windows that keep us from seeing the world.

God calls you to a journey

God wants you to keep moving and going into new territory with God and with other people. The world and its needs are ahead of you on your road, waiting for you. God is there waiting for you, too. Unfortunately, rather than continuing to travel with God many of us choose to settle down permanently at a comfortable spot along the way. We're willing to go only so far and no farther. Then God has to go on without us.

We treat our churches like roadside condominiums in which we can establish ownership and then rest in comfort and safety while other people make the journey. From our secure vantage point as spectators we then feel free to criticize and advise the travelers as they pass by. Jesus described his mission, and therefore ours, as something very different.

The church needs to be a roadside place where travelers and their guides can be fed, trained, informed, refreshed, healed, and encouraged in order to get back out onto the road with God. The church can't afford to be a place where members settle down for a permanent rest.

In one way the church is no different from the world: the people in the church are human, which means they're a mixture of good and evil just as the people outside the church are. They are struck by disasters just as the people outside the church are. They treat themselves and others unkindly at times and kindly at other times, just as people outside the church do.

In a very important way, however, the church is different. The church has accepted the God-given responsibility for demonstrating a way of reacting to disaster and unkindness that is different from the world's way. We've also taken on the job of teaching and, even more important, of modeling a way of treating people that is different from the world's way.

The church has become aware of a better way, which the Bible calls the kingdom of God. It's the way the world would function if everyone let God have complete authority over their lives. Two thousand years ago God sent Jesus to show the world what that better way would look like in a real human life, and God calls us to continue the job.

When we take this responsibility seriously, there's no doubt about who needs the church. Everyone does. The whole world needs it desperately.

Questions for Reflection

1. When have you ever had occasion to think of yourself with a new title or name? Was it difficult to make the change?

2. If you are active in a church, how does your church encourage you to try to find out what God is calling you to do, and to re-

spond? As an individual, how might you help others recognize and respond to God's call?

3. How does your church help you to recognize your gifts and put them to full use? How might you help your church do this better for all its members?

4. If you are a church member, what promises did you make when you became a member? How might you carry them out more fully?

5. Does large attendance at a certain church or church program show that the program reflects God's will? If not, what would show that?

6. How would Jeremiah be received as a member of your church or of your circle of friends?

7. What's the difference between church members and non-members? Why should anyone be a member?

8. If you're active in a church, what does your church do to help outsiders see what God is like when they look at the church? What does it do to help its members look out and see the world's needs? How might you help these things to happen more often?

9. How does your church keep people feeling like outsiders? How could you help change this?

10. How do you feel about Barbara's view of traditional church practices and the need for change?

11. What other feelings or thoughts came to you as you read Barbara's comments about the church?

Chapter 6

What Will Happen?

Barbara: God Will Keep Doing Exciting New Things

In the Bible you find the phrases "kingdom of God" and "kingdom of heaven" used to describe what the world would be like if everyone followed God's will perfectly. God's kingdom is the ultimate picture of a world where God and all of God's creation are in harmony. It is ultimate in the sense of last in a time-ordered sequence, and also in the sense of the greatest imaginable—the peak, the maximum, the best. The kingdom of God is the greatest, and it has something to do with the end of time. In the Gospels Jesus tells people "the kingdom of God is within you" or "among you" (Luke 17:21, NIV) and describes it as the best way of living—God's way, in contrast to the world's way. In other places Jesus speaks of the kingdom as something that will happen at the end of human history (Matthew 7:21-23 and 13:47-50).

Sometimes you find these two meanings brought together, as when Paul calls Jesus the "first fruit" of the kingdom (1 Corinthians 15:20). He is like the very first peach that you find on a peach tree in your yard; it shows you what will eventually come from the whole tree. It's like getting a sample of a new product in the mail: the manufacturer sends it to you thinking that you'll like it well enough to want more.

Jesus brought the world the first tiny glimpse of something huge that would eventually be more widely available. Then he gave his followers the job of making more of it available. As Jesus' follower you are to be part of a much larger sample of the kingdom of God. Jesus was the first fruit and his followers are the later fruits, who show the world what human life and relationships are like when people live in the way that God wants them to live.

That's a large order! Living the way everybody else in the world does is easier and more comfortable than being a living sample of God's way. For this reason most of us go along with ruthless tactics to get what we want. We empower some groups of people and keep others powerless, and we try to justify what we're doing by saying, "That's just the way the world is." We overlook the fact that we're here not to help the world stay the way it is but to help it become more like the kingdom of God. That means doing things a different way from the way everybody else usually does them.

The kingdom of God is power

The New Testament says a lot about what the kingdom of God is like. Many of the descriptions have become well known: the kingdom is like a tiny seed that can become a huge tree (Matthew 13:31-32); it is like a valuable pearl (Matthew 13:45-46); it is like yeast in bread dough (Matthew 13:33); it is like buried treasure (Matthew 13:44). But there's another description that hasn't become so well known: "The kingdom of God does not consist in talk but in power" (1 Corinthians 4:20, RSV). Many people tend to think about the kingdom of God as an airy, unreal place where angelic beings waft around wearing halos and playing harps and looking pious. But here is Paul saying that the kingdom consists of power, which is a down-to-earth feature of ordinary life right here in the world. In fact, it's something we often think of as evil or at least inappropriate for Christians to want. The catch to Paul's statement is that the power that is a feature of the kingdom of God, while it is not at all airy or unreal, is different from the power that we know best.

Some contemporary thinkers have observed that power comes in different forms. The power that we see most is often described as "power over." It is dominating power, in which someone gives the orders and enforces them, and someone else has no choice but to follow them, and the two people or groups never trade places. In order for you to have this kind of power over me, I must be kept powerless; only one of us can have power.

This kind of power operates in a hierarchy—a pecking order, like a ladder on which each person or group has permanent power over everyone below them. "Power over" requires making perfectly clear who's in charge, and keeping that person or group in charge. In this kind of set-up you stay in power by flexing your muscles or rattling your guns or reminding people of your big bank account—by letting people know that you are stronger than they are and that you won't hesitate to use your strength to keep them in line if they don't stay there voluntarily. Using this kind of power means imposing your will on others.

The power that characterizes the kingdom of God is different. It is "power to." It is simply the ability to accomplish something. It's the power to get a job done. You can have power to do something, and so can I; your having power doesn't require me to stay powerless. I'm not just a tool that you use for exerting your power. Many people can have "power to" at the same time without interfering with each other. It's more like a circle than a ladder. When you see people using "power to" you're seeing a sample of the kingdom of God.

Prophetic voices reveal the kingdom of God

Throughout human history God has provided prophetic voices to point out what God's way was for a particular situation. God's prophets have always helped people to see the kingdom of God in their midst and to see how it differed from the world's way that was currently in use. Prophets are people to whom God has given special ability to see what others aren't seeing. God also gives prophets the ability to communicate what they see. Prophetic voices speak for God.

God puts prophetic voices in strategic positions in the church and the world and enables them to speak out, communicating God's word to their fellow human beings. God calls the rest of us to listen for these prophetic voices and to act on what they are saying. God wants us to recognize them as God's spokespersons and to pay attention to what they are seeing and saying, even if we can't see what they see.

When we fail to heed what the prophetic voices in our midst are saying, we're making the same mistake as the people whom Old Testament prophets and Jesus often criticized: harsh kings and their underlings; greedy business and political leaders who lorded it over less powerful citizens; and self-righteous religious leaders who presided over worship in the temple and its related local shrines. Throughout the Bible you can read about prophets who urged these leaders to change their ways, to follow God's way instead of the world's way. But unfortunately many of the prophets were ignored and disaster struck.

We see the same process happening today in our churches and

our world. Our long-established ways become so comfortably familiar that we assume they are God's way when they're not. It doesn't
occur to us to question them, especially if they're benefiting us. We
can't even imagine any alternatives, but God always knows alternatives and reveals them to people within every situation, including
ours. Our job is to recognize the prophetic voices among us and to
act on what they are saying, even if it threatens our own comfort,
status, and security.

Recognizing God's prophets isn't always easy. Plenty of people
claim to be God-inspired but aren't. Plenty of people rebel and criticize the status quo without being God's prophets. Trying to recognize legitimate prophets is like trying to be sure the compulsions you
feel are coming from the Holy Spirit. You have to evaluate prophets
by asking for God's help, comparing their message to the overall
message of the Bible, collecting opinions from a variety of other
Christians, and using various spiritual disciplines to help you focus
on God and interpret what you are reading, hearing, and thinking.
Then you must decide and act in accordance with your decision,
knowing that you may be wrong. And you can't stop there; you'll
have to stay on the lookout for more information and stay open to
new insight, knowing that you may need to revise your decision.

You can find plenty of reasons to ignore prophetic voices. They
may be calling for change that would make you uncomfortable, giving you a strong motive for claiming that they are wrong. Since it's
not easy to distinguish true prophets from other people who claim to
be prophets, sometimes it seems safer just to ignore them.

There's another problem, too. Prophetic voices often come from
unexpected people who don't look or act like you think God's messengers should. Throughout history God's prophets have often been
people on the fringes of their society, rarely holding the traditional
leadership roles. This isn't surprising, because the people who are
best at envisioning new possibilities are rarely the same people who
are satisfied with administering established systems and following
standard procedures.

So prophets are usually nonconformists. They may in fact be
rebels and misfits in the view of most people around them. They
don't help to preserve the status quo; they criticize it instead, just as
Jesus did when he pronounced judgment on many customs of his
day. He presented alternatives that many of his listeners evidently

thought were heretical or at least hopelessly impractical, just as we often do when we hear today's prophetic voices. But we need to hear them and pay attention even if it hurts—even if they suggest giving up cherished parts of our churches, our governmental institutions, or our lifestyles that don't conform to God's will.

To become the life-changing and world-changing disciple that God calls you to be, you'll have to heed what today's prophetic voices are saying. If you happen to be called to be one of those voices yourself, you'll have to speak out bravely even if it makes you unpopular.

Some of today's prophetic voices undoubtedly belong to women who once felt, as I did, that God required us to stay silent, invisible, and powerless, doing only supportive jobs in the background of life while men represented us in the church and the world. Many of us now realize that this role was prescribed only by our society, not by God, and we are ready to step out from the background and speak for ourselves or even speak for God if God calls and enables us to do so. Will our church and our world hear us? Or will they keep trying to stifle us because we're advocating change that threatens the comfort and security of those who have been able to exert power over us for so long in the past?

What about the voices of other formerly silent people in our church and our world? What about people from nonwhite races, Third World countries, and the poorest segments of society? Are we willing to hear them when they cry out in pain or in judgment? God's prophets have often come from marginal groups like these, so it's not surprising if they do today.

Prophets urge us to think and act in new ways

For many centuries prophetic leaders have been reminding us that God intends for us to keep growing and changing, and that God wants us to live in a way that is noticeably different from the way of the world around us. Paul said it this way: "Do not conform yourselves to the standards of this world, but let God transform you inwardly by a complete change of your mind. Then you will be able to know the will of God . . ." (Romans 12:2, GNB).

In our own day prophetic voices are urging Christians to take a fresh look at ourselves, our churches, our Christian tradition, and our world, and to let God transform our understanding. Speaking for

God, these voices are asking us to notice what the Bible shows about God's actions toward humankind and to cooperate with what God is doing in today's world.

It won't be exactly what God did yesterday or last year or in earlier centuries. It will have the same purpose, but it will involve new tactics, because new conditions keep arising and the old methods are no longer suitable. To see what God is doing we have to look ahead, not back. God made this clear long ago when he said through the prophet Isaiah, "Do not cling to events of the past or dwell on what happened long ago. Watch for the new thing I am going to do. It is happening already—you can see it now!" (Isaiah 43:18-19, GNB).

The God of history is not asking you to copy what the church has done in the past or even what Jesus said and did during his time on earth. Instead, God is calling you to be part of Christ's body in ways that fit your own time and place. Doing that won't necessarily be easy. It may mean knowingly choosing a hard and dangerous road. But you'll have a journey that is full of exciting surprises as well as difficulties and dangers. God will go with you, guiding you, helping you, and cheering you on when the going gets hard. Without the assurance that God will go with you and enable you to do what needs doing, you could never summon the nerve to start out or to keep going, but with God's help you can. Contemporary theologian Denise Carmody puts it like this:

> To embark on a spiritual journey is to place oneself in a certain peril, a certain surety of meeting dragons. The only way to keep going, not give up when one sees what beasts inhabit one's own depths as well as the jungles of the world, is to believe that one's God has commanded the quest.[1]

Your God *has* commanded the quest. As part of the body of Christ for today, the Spirit of God is upon you whether you are lay or clergy. God's Spirit can enable you to proclaim good news, recovery of sight, and freedom to those who are poor, blind, and oppressed in your everyday surroundings. Whenever and wherever this happens, the kingdom of God is present.

In the book of Revelation you can read a description of the New

---

1. Denise Lardner Carmody, *Seizing the Apple: A Feminist Spirituality of Personal Growth* (New York: Crossroad, 1984), 177-178.

Jerusalem, a symbolic way of picturing God's kingdom. One thing about it may surprise you: there is no temple. God and Jesus are the temple (21:22). Another passage, which has become well known through Handel's oratorio *The Messiah*, explains further: "The kingdom of the world has become the kingdom of our Lord and of his Christ" (Revelation 11:15, NIV). Like the role of parents in their children's lives, the role of the church and its tradition is to become unnecessary.

Someone has said that tradition is the living faith of the dead, while traditionalism is the dead faith of the living. Tradition can play a valuable part in your life if you see it properly as a collection of landmarks and road signs along your route to the new destinations that God is leading you toward. However, if you let tradition become your destination—a stopping point—then it becomes traditionalism and it is deadly instead of enlivening. It makes religious institutions, symbols, and practices into idols.They become museum pieces instead of helpful guides, walls instead of the windows that God intends them to be.

The church is to serve as a sample of the kingdom of God now, but when its job is done, what began as a mere sample will have grown to fill the entire world—the entire cosmos, in fact. This is the ultimate that God has in mind. The Bible says that hell will not be able to destroy the church (Matthew 16:18), but this doesn't mean that God will not allow the church to come to an end when it has served its purpose.

God's ultimate is always beyond us

The Bible often pictures the kingdom of God in terms of the end of time. As a result, all through history people have tried to outguess God about when the end of time and God's final judgment will take place, even though Jesus warns us not to expect to be able to figure it out. Jesus refused to answer some people who were trying to get him to tell them when to expect his second coming and the end of time. In fact, he said that even he didn't have the answer. "No one knows about that day or hour, not even the angels in heaven, nor the Son," he told them, "but only the Father" (Matthew 24:36, NIV).

Our job as Christians in today's world is to go where God leads us, and God won't lead us all to the same place. God calls some of us to serve within the institutional church and others to go out and be the scattered church serving in the world. God calls some of us to be prophets—to be the brave people who speak up and say that the emperor really doesn't have on any clothes even if others insist that he does. God calls others of us to recognize and heed the prophetic voices that speak for God. God doesn't call anybody to just sit and do nothing. That's probably the worst thing you can do. God apparently says, "Make your best effort to find out what I want you to do, and then do it, even though you risk being wrong."

In the book of Revelation you can read about the kind of church that does nothing. It's described as a lukewarm church, and God doesn't have anything good to say about it. God tells this church, "You say, 'I am rich; I have acquired wealth and do not need a thing.' But you do not realize that you are wretched, pitiful, poor, blind and naked." God tells this church, "because you are lukewarm—neither hot nor cold—I am about to spit you out of my mouth" (3:16-17, NIV). Some scholars say that the real connotation of the original Greek words is, "You make me want to throw up!" But God doesn't leave even the blah church without hope. Jesus says, "Listen! I am standing at the door, knocking; if you hear my voice and open the door, I will come in to you and eat with you, and you with me" (Revelation 3:20, NRSV).

Walt Whitman once said of Ralph Waldo Emerson, "I was simmering, and he brought me to a boil." Maybe that's what Christians need someone to do for them now. If we're only lukewarm, we need the heat turned up before we can even simmer! If we're lukewarm, we're still a long way from the boiling point, where things start cooking and real transformation begins.

As fellow Christians we need to turn up the heat under one another, warming up those who are cold, starting the lukewarm ones to simmer, and bringing the simmering ones to a boil. We can do this by helping one another recognize our God-given gifts and the ministries to which God is calling us. Then we can support and hold one another accountable as we travel along the road with God.

I hope that this book has turned up the heat a little for you. Jesus can't come in and eat with you until you get something cooking.

Questions for Reflection

1. What are some examples of "power over" and "power to" that you can see in your life and in our society?

2. What prophetic voices are speaking for God in today's world? Can you recognize some on the national and international levels? in your church or home town? What makes you think they are speaking for God? How do you react to them?

3. Do you agree with Barbara's suggestions about how to recognize God's true prophets? What suggestions would you add?

4. Have you ever felt called to speak for God? In what circumstances? How did you respond? If you spoke, what results could you see?

5. Do you understand God to be mainly calling Christians forward to try new ways or back to maintain old ones? What evidence do you see that supports your view?

6. Have you become aware of some "beasts that inhabit your own depths as well as the jungles of the world"? If so, how has this awareness affected your response to God's call?

7. How do you feel about the idea that the church may not last forever?

8. Has anyone brought you to a boil when you were simmering? If so, how did it happen, and what did you do as a result?

9. What other feelings or thoughts came to you as you read Barbara's discussion of the kingdom of God?

What Will Happen?
Stan: God's Way Will Become the World's Way

Your days may be filled with stress. You have a lot of things to get done and there's no way you can do them all. All you can do is keep trying to do whichever one can't be put off any longer. Then, as if you didn't have enough to do already, people keep trying to get you to take on volunteer jobs and to help all kinds of causes that might make your local community and the world a better place. You're constantly under pressure.

Or you may face the opposite problem. You feel as if you're merely existing, and you're not sure why you continue to live. The days seem endless. You can't see any hope of tomorrow being any different from today, and it makes you want to give up on life.

Or perhaps your life is stable right now. Things seem to be going all right. At the same time, you sense that there should be more to life than just having this good fortune. You may wonder if you can help others, but you are not sure what you should do to help. You experience some stirrings of the spirit to take advantage of your circumstances to explore life's mysteries, but you sense that the needed response may not be to just get busy doing things.

Whatever your current situation may be, you need a vision of what God wants the world to be. The only way you can make reasonable choices from among all the available options is by knowing what is finally important to God. You need to know about God's "last things."

If you're too busy, you may think that's the kind of impractical suggestion that only a person with no conception of the real world would make. "Here I am, up to my ears in work, with the boss and the bank breathing down my neck: what do God's 'last things' have to do with my real life? I don't even know what that means." On the other hand, if you're wishing for more to fill your time, you're probably thinking, "What difference does the vague, distant future make? The only thing that would help me would be something concrete that I could do *today* – something that would really matter."

What difference do God's "last things" make?

Even if you're an active churchgoer you probably don't hear much about what the church has traditionally called "last things." "Last things," as the church understands them, are the kingdom of God, the last judgment, the second coming of Christ, the resurrection of the body, and eternal life. If you attend a church that uses the Apostles' Creed regularly, you hear about the resurrection of the body, and you probably hear about eternal life on Easter, but these certainly aren't everyday words. Every now and then a group is in the news for claiming that the second coming and the last judgment are about to happen, usually when something that's currently happening in the Middle East looks like something that the book of Revelation describes. Sometimes one of these groups even goes out to a mountaintop to wait for Jesus to come and take them to heaven, since they think they know when he's coming.

This kind of anticipation doesn't mean much. It has been happening regularly for the two thousand years since Jesus' death. There's always some group that thinks they have God's timetable figured out, but they've been wrong every time. So why would you want to spend much time thinking about this kind of "last things"? They don't seem to have much to do with everyday life in the real world.

Christians in the early church thought about the kingdom of God and the last judgment a lot, because they expected Jesus to return during their lifetimes. You can see this in several books of the New Testament. As time went by and Jesus didn't come back, these early Christians began to realize that they needed to start thinking about how to live in this world for the long run. Jesus evidently wasn't going to come and snatch them out of it in time to solve their day-to-day problems. If the kingdom of God wasn't going to arrive in full force right away, Christians had to start thinking about what to do next in their everyday life.

Jesus had told them, of course, that they were not to be mere passive spectators. He had prayed for God's kingdom to come, but he also had said plenty about what his followers were to do while they waited for it. When they realized what this meant, the picture of God's kingdom became a source of energy for them. It helped them to go about the business of everyday life with a new sense of direction, worth, and purpose.

Living with the kingdom of God as their model enabled the early Christians to change the world. Throughout the centuries since then, having a clear picture of the "last things" has helped Christians to see the "next things" that needed to be done and has furnished the motivation they needed for doing them.

So for us, too, God's "last things" are vitally important, for only they can give us the perspective and stamina we need for what needs to be done right now.

Does death mean life is meaningless?

Death is your future. That's discouraging to have to think about, isn't it? You may try to deny death or postpone it or ignore it, but you can't avoid it forever. Sometimes it's even hard to avoid right now; you keep coming across daily reminders that you are fighting a losing battle. Work that you did yesterday has to be done again today. You look in the mirror and see wrinkles and bulges that weren't there until recently. You get out of breath now when you try to walk up stairs that you once could climb easily. The roof on your house suddenly springs a leak. And these are only the small reminders!

At best, your efforts are merely a holding action. Your victories are temporary. The forces of death keep reasserting themselves, showing you again and again that nothing you do can change this basic fact of life. Even if you have great power now, death roams the halls. You will have to turn loose of your power someday, and that time may not be far away.

Maybe a solution to the problem of death would be to put a higher priority on relationships and good deeds than on power. If you joined your life with others to do something lasting, at least you could be remembered for it. Yet all you have to do is to walk through an old, forgotten cemetery to see that this strategy doesn't really solve the problem. Nor does placing your trust in your mind: for a few creative people, the more durable world of ideas seems to offer a way to outwit death. But even ideas have their day and then new ideas replace them. Artifacts like paintings or literature may last the longest, but nothing we create or collect will last forever.

If death has the last word, is your life a mere "trivial pursuit"? Faith says it is much more than that. Faith says that death doesn't have to be seen as the enemy of meaning. Death is the enemy only because it reminds you that all of your attempts at self-preservation are bound to fail.

Much of what human beings do is done in an effort to restrain death, even though much of it isn't recognized as having this aim. Your efforts may seem to work for a while. You can expand some boundaries in order to hold back the forces that oppose you. You can be energized temporarily by your attempts to avoid meaninglessness, whether you do it by trying to preserve the status quo or by being part of the avant-garde.

These superficial efforts to find outer security and inner meaning aren't what God intends for your life. God wants you to know that Christ's resurrection has broken death's power over your life and given you a new reason for courage. This doesn't mean, of course, that your physical life will not end. Instead, it means that your life will be fulfilled. It can have meaning. God promises this to you.

Your work is evidence of God's promise. You have been created as God's partner in order to do God's work in God's world. The resurrection lets you know that your work and your life both count. A Latin American Christian wrote in prison that the first Easter morning, the day of Christ's resurrection is "the day which can no longer be denied us."[1]

Because of the resurrection the threat that death brings by pointing to the failure of your work is no longer decisive. You can live with the courage that comes from the resurrection, because in it God promises you that your work for others and for the world has meaning. Death's threatening word is not the last word about your work. The last word is God's, and it is a word of life and meaning.

Paul expressed the significance of the resurrection for living the life of faith in his second letter to the Corinthians:

> Hard-pressed on every side, we are never hemmed in; bewildered, we are never at our wits' end; hunted, we are never

---

1. Lochman, *The Faith We Confess*, 248.

abandoned to our fate; struck down, we are not left to die.
Wherever we go we carry death with us in our body, the death
that Jesus died, that in this body also life may reveal itself, the
life that Jesus lives. (2 Corinthians 4:8-10, NEB)

God's judgment is also a promise

You live under judgment. One place you experience it is in
your work, for that is where people judge you. The people you
serve judge you, those you work with judge you, those you work
for judge you, and you judge yourself. Everything you do is judged
by someone.

As a believer you know that the last judgment is God's, and that
can make you uneasy. You know that the record will show ques-
tionable motives, less-than-perfect actions, and mixed results. Even
if your work has usually been praised, you keep feeling that you
could have done more and better.

But God's judgment is also a promise. Both its intention and its
outcome have the same aim: restoring you to a life lived as God's
partner. Being God's partner means living in a helpful community
in harmony with God and your neighbors. God, therefore, judges
your work on the basis of how it creates, promotes, and nurtures
community.

Jesus tells the story of the last judgment in order to show you
that even your smallest and most casual contacts with others are
part of a divine drama. In this drama God invites you to recognize
and respond to Christ in your neighbor. Your neighbor is the one
through whom you can serve Jesus the Christ.

Once you have heard Jesus' call, you can live by a new set of
values—the values that are on the other side of judgment. You see
that faithfulness is not measured by how near the top of the ladder
you climb in your chosen vocation. It is measured instead by the
way in which you used the opportunities to serve others that your
vocation provided. Love is not discouraged by the opinions of
people who tell you that you are foolish when you try to serve
others and measure your success by this standard. You don't have
to be impressed when people say you should put your own interests first. You have seen how futile that strategy will turn out to be
in the long run.

With this vision of God's judgment you find that God's provi-
dence becomes important for you. God promises to provide what

you need, and this means God won't abandon you. It means you are free to go about your work as God's partner, caring for God's world. You are free to care for others – even your enemies – because you know that God cares for you.

Your confidence comes from knowing that God's kingdom will never end. You know that you are serving a love that can't be conquered, because it changes even the defeats in your life into victories of faith. God's gift of love gives you the courage that you need to live and work every day for the coming kingdom. You know that the judgment that counts comes from God, who shows you what it means to live a life of love.

Love is patient; love is kind and envies no one. Love is never boastful, nor conceited, nor rude; never selfish, not quick to take offence. Love keeps no score of wrongs; does not gloat over [others'] sins, but delights in the truth. There is nothing love cannot face; there is no limit to its faith, its hope, and its endurance. (1 Corinthians 13:4-7, NEB)

The promise of Christ's return

The promised return of Christ means that God's values didn't just apply to a time in the distant past. They're the values that apply for all time, and Christ will reappear at the end of time to reconfirm them. What we call the "real world" has gotten everything out of order, but when Christ returns the real world that God intended will be established. The good news that in God's kingdom everyone is invited, welcomed, and given equal status will become a universal reality, because Christ died for all.

The promise of Christ's second coming, therefore, sets new standards by which you can measure your life and work. Five standards can be your guides. First, your choices must put God's will ahead of your will. Next, you must recognize that the main purpose of your vocation is to serve others. Third, your work must bring you into community with others and express your solidarity with them. Fourth, your actions must aim at mercy and kindness rather than vengeance. God wants you to help those who have failed find a new future. And last, you must place love before justice, because your efforts to achieve justice will never be completely just. The aim of the second coming of Jesus is not to banish and punish. It is to restore. It is to show that the kingdom of God is a universal kingdom.

The image of the second coming of Christ is full of irony and surprise. It purifies as well as confirms; it purges as well as heals. At the second coming the humble will be exalted and the exalted will be humbled. When you look at the image of the second coming, you see that your daily work and your life struggles are more serious than they seem at first glance. Your work is not just a way to make a living; it is a way to make a life of love and faith. Meister Eckhart, a thirteenth-century German Christian, said, "Work does not make us holy. Instead, we must make the work holy."[2] This is just as true for the accountant or politician as it was for the scholarly monk Eckhart, and just as true in the twentieth century as it was in the thirteenth.

The book of Revelation describes the vision of "a new heaven and a new earth" that God revealed to one of Jesus' followers. This image shows God's promise of the second coming in its true light, for the second coming brings radical change. God says, "See, I am making all things new" (Revelation 21:1,5, NRSV).

This radical change doesn't mean you will move from a world of work to a world of leisure and rest. Work is not the mark of the old order; the mark of the old order is work plagued by brokenness, strife, sorrow, fear, hatred, despair, and anxiety. In the new age that God promises, that burden of the old age is lifted. You can live now with the assurance that God who has begun a new kind of life in you and your work will fulfill it.

So in the light of the second coming the purpose of your work becomes clear. In your work, you are Christ's agent of reconciliation. You don't give in to the forces that bring suffering to you and to others. Therefore, your suffering doesn't have to cause despair. You can see your suffering as evidence of your worth. You can rejoice even when people say all kinds of ugly things about you for trying to do what God is calling you to do (Matthew 5:11).

In the sense that you choose to do your work even though it stirs up opposition and causes you to suffer, your work is your cross, which Jesus says you must take up daily if you are to be one of his followers (Matthew 10:38, Mark 8:34, Luke 9:23 and 14:27). This doesn't mean that you merely have to put up with inconven-

---

2. Quoted in Carl Michalson, *Faith for Personal Crises* (New York: Charles Scribner's Sons, 1958), 111.

iences and problems in the course of doing your work. It means that your suffering, when you see that your work always falls short and that you may be attacked for doing it, is similar to what Jesus experienced. Jesus' sorrow is truly yours, and yours is also his. But most important of all, this also means that his joy is now yours as well. This joy is the real promise of Christ's second coming.

His purpose in dying for all was that [human beings], while still in life, should cease to live for themselves, and should live for him who for their sake died and was raised to life. . . . When anyone is united to Christ, there is a new world; the old order has gone, and a new order has already begun. (2 Corinthians 5:15-17, NEB)

Eternal life is a way of living now

Eternal life is more than life after death. It is a quality of living now. We see evidence of this kind of life when people act on the basis of faith's promise that glimpses of the kingdom of God can break into the present and change it, from a peasants' revolt in Luther's time and the resistance to colonialism to the American civil rights movement and various liberation movements that are happening all over the world. Whether you agree with the exact aims of these movements or not, you can see that they arose because people saw that their present situation wasn't the only way to live.

Although some optimistic views of progress seem naive, the image of the kingdom of God shows that the world can and should be different. Advocates of change don't have to be utopians with their heads in the clouds. It is true that you can't afford to underestimate the powers of darkness, but it is also true that you cannot afford to ignore the call to serve the power of light.

One danger that you face when you answer the call is that you will become disenchanted because of past experience with promises that turned out to be unreliable, or with hopes that didn't pan out. When this attitude gets the best of you, you despair of being able to accomplish anything.

A greater temptation, however, is to believe that you can actually get rid of evil by what you do. Evil is overcome only through Christ's suffering, and only Christ can help you to remember this and to receive the wisdom that you need to be able to live with your hopes.

If you try to define good in terms of your self-interest, you will fail to see how you often serve your interests at the expense of other people. The good is too often defined as what is good for me. So when you try to accomplish what you think will be good, other people protest and claim that your vision is faulty. As you live with this kind of frustration, you become less sure of your ability to know what good is, and still less to do it. Then you have a hard time remembering that eternal life and the perfection that it represents must be received as God's gift; you can't achieve them by your own efforts.

One of the gifts of eternal life is a new freedom—the freedom to care. You can no longer be indifferent. You stand *with* other people, not against them. "Eternal life is the real secret of this temporal life," Karl Barth observes. "We do not yet live eternal life here and now. But we are here and now made free for eternal life."[3]

Eternal life secures the meaning of your life by connecting it to the risen Christ who returns. Because the basis of your faith rests on this secure foundation, neither the surprises of the world's history nor the unpredictable parts of your own life can dislodge you. You may be called foolish, but this won't matter. Others may ignore you or even reject you, but this is not what matters. The meaning of your life is secure, and that's what matters.

Eternal life is mystery. You don't hold it; it holds you. You no longer live on a treadmill in your daily work or feel that the next step in the relay race of history is totally up to you. Eternal life promises that your life and work are neither pointless nor ineffective. Instead, they have meaning in their own right, regardless of how other people assess them. Paul describes this kind of life in his first letter to the Corinthians:

> We are fools for Christ's sake. . . . We are weak. . . . We are in disgrace. . . . To this day we go hungry and thirsty and in rags; we are roughly handled; we wander from place to place; we wear ourselves out working with our own hands. They curse us, and we bless; they persecute us, and we submit to it; they slander us, and we humbly make our appeal. . . . The kingdom of God is not a matter of talk, but of power. (1 Corinthians 4:10-13, 20, NEB)

---

3. Barth, *Church Dogmatics*, 2/2:773-74.

The kingdom of God means change

When you try to live from and for the kingdom of God, change comes. It comes, first, because the world is not what God intends it to be, and second, because God can turn intentions into reality. What you can't even imagine, God can do. For this reason, it has often been said that the kingdom of God is beyond history. This doesn't mean you can give up on your responsibilities; it means that you aim at a goal that is beyond you. You live for God's kingdom, in the presence of God.

The future belongs only to God. All other claims about it are unreliable. Human reformers can rearrange the furniture, but they can't build a new house. No human being can engineer the transformation that the world longs for. But your work has a place in the transformation that God is bringing about, so you can't afford to become a skeptic.

You simply know that the world is free to be the world; you can't claim anything else for it. It is not to be the object of worship; it is to be the subject of your service. When you look at the world from the perspective of the kingdom of God, you live in the world under new rules. You know that your vocation is to be God's partner and to serve as a midwife who helps bring forth God's kingdom. You worship God and care for the world.

You also share God's work. As contemporary theologian Jürgen Moltmann points out, "God does not want the humility of servants or the gratitude of children for ever. [God] wants the boldness and confidence of friends, who share his rule with him."[4] Misunderstanding this view of God could lead to harmful spiritual arrogance, however, so you face a dilemma. Theologian Rosemary Radford Ruether expresses its essence:

> When men tailor their hopes to the presently possible, their accomplishments will surely fall far behind, yet the vision of radical and sweeping renewal spins off into empty frustration unless it does mesh in a practical way with matter and in their interaction, the word to some extent becomes flesh.[5]

---

4. Jürgen Moltmann, The Trinity and the Kingdom (New York: Harper and Row, 1981), 221.
5. Rosemary Radford Ruether, The Radical Kingdom (New York: Paulist Press, 1970), 286.

This is the reality of the life of faith: to live from the kingdom of God is to be an agent of judgment in the world. Whether you pray for the world to change, disclaim the value of its rewards and punishments, or try to change it yourself, you are saying that the world is not what it should and could be. When you try to be faithful to the vision of God's kingdom, you can't help seeing the shortcomings of your work. Like the rest of creation, you yourself stand under judgment and need mercy. You must trust God's mercy while you work for God's kingdom. God's promise of the kingdom gives you permission to keep expressing Jesus' vocation in your everyday life. God keeps reminding you that "you may," "you can," and "you will," and each affirmation is followed by a resounding "amen." The promise is fulfilled, and it is still being fulfilled. As Paul says,

We wield the weapons of righteousness in right hand and left. Honour and dishonour, praise and blame, are alike our lot: we are the impostors who speak the truth, the unknown [people] whom all [others] know; dying we still live on; disciplined by suffering, we are not done to death; in our sorrows we have always cause for joy; poor ourselves, we bring wealth to many; penniless, we own the world. (2 Corinthians 6:7-10, NEB)

Living from and for God's kingdom

In his book, *Marie*, Peter Maas tells about someone who lived from and for the kingdom of God.[6] Marie Ragghianti grew up in a traditional Roman Catholic family. In high school she was a beauty queen caught up in the glamour of clothes and good-looking boys. Immediately after graduation she married the handsome football star, and soon she was the mother of two sons and a daughter.

Her marriage didn't work out. In moods of depression her husband would often abuse her and threaten her with a knife, but leaving him wasn't easy; it wasn't what women did in the world Marie lived in. Still, Marie felt she had to leave. She feared for her children's lives as well as her own.

Soon after Marie and the children went on their own, one of the boys swallowed a pistachio nutshell that went into his lung. For months he had spells of being almost unable to breathe, and Marie

---

6. Peter Maas, *Marie* (New York: Pocket Books, 1983).

would rush him to the hospital. Though at times he was on the verge of death, doctors could not locate the nutshell that was causing the problem and even doubted Marie's story. Finally, they located the nutshell and removed it.

Marie was forced to live in poor housing because she had little money, but she decided to go to college. During her last year in college she worked for the Democratic party, helping to elect a new governor for her state. Soon after the election she was offered a job in the state government, dealing with paroles. Every now and then she saw some things happening that she didn't think were right, and she reported them to the governor's assistant who had arranged the job for her.

Later she was put on the state's three-person parole board and was even made its chairperson. The more she saw of the board's operation, the more things she found that were not right. She kept reporting them, but she was always told not to worry and was reminded that she needed the job to support her family.

Finally, she became convinced that the problem was too serious to overlook any longer. She went to the F.B.I. Soon one of her colleagues who had been helping her collect evidence was found murdered, so Marie began to take precautions. She feared for her life. When her allegations became public, the governor ordered her to back down, but she refused. She believed in the democratic system of government and was confident that right would win in the end.

One evening she was arrested after having had a glass of wine at a party, and was falsely charged with being drunk. The false charge had to be dropped, but her reputation was seriously damaged. The governor removed her from office, claiming that she had misused state funds.

Marie decided to challenge him in court. There were now nine charges against her, and to win her case she would have to be acquitted on all nine. She was. In the end the governor and his assistant were tried and found guilty of corruption in arranging parole for state prison inmates. Many friends complimented Marie on her courage, but she was told that she would never hold another job in the state government. Throughout this process Marie attended mass each morning and went on frequent retreats. She felt sure that she had to keep challenging what she saw as wrong, even at great cost to herself.

Marie believed in God's promises. Her decisions about how to handle the next step in her daily life, even when her life was in danger, were always based on her vision of God's kingdom. She looked death in the face three times, in the form of her husband's abuse, her child's illness, and the revenge that her opponents tried to carry out against her when she kept standing up for what she believed. Each time, she found that God's promises about the "last things" gave her the strength and the determination she needed for dealing with the "next thing" she had to do in her daily life. As a result, this one vulnerable woman did what others had not succeeded in doing, even though they seemed to have more power and opportunity than she did.

God's "last things" let you know that God intends for you to be a real partner—to do God's work for the world, to be God's friend, to use your God-given gifts for the world's benefit, and to show that God's promise to the world can be trusted. Every minute of every day you live in the presence of God's promised kingdom, and your works don't just point to that kingdom. They make it possible.

Questions for Reflection

1. How can having a clear vision of God's "last things" help you with the "next things" you need to do?

2. What reminders of death concern you the most? How do you try to postpone death or avoid it?

3. To what extent does knowing that your life has meaning keep you from being discouraged by the failures, suffering, and criticism that you experience in everyday life?

4. How do you feel about facing God's judgment?

5. What keeps you from feeling free to go about your work as God's partner, caring for others and serving them?

6. How would you do your daily work differently if you applied the five standards of putting God's will first, serving others, bringing you into community with others, aiming at mercy and kindness, and placing love before justice?

7. Do you agree that "your work is not just a way to make a living; it is a way to make a life of love and faith"?

8. Stan mentions several movements of groups that have worked for change, which he sees as evidence of eternal life breaking into the present. What evidence of eternal life do you see in your world right now?

9. Does being called foolish, being ignored and rejected, and being mistreated matter to you? How do you feel about Stan's saying that they don't matter when one's faith rests on the secure foundation of eternal life?

10. In what way are you serving as "a midwife who helps bring forth God's kingdom"? How might you begin doing so in a new way?

11. Where could you find the support you need for doing what you find God calling you to do?

12. What other questions, thoughts, and feelings came to you as you read Stan's discussion of God's "last things"?

Conclusion
You Can Fill in the Blanks

It's up to you. God has left some blanks that only you can fill, and God has given you the freedom to choose whether or not you will fill them. God wants them filled, but if you choose not to fill them they will stay unfilled.

At the same time, it's not up to you. God will keep calling you, nudging you forward – even tugging you forward at times – and encouraging you to keep going when you're tempted to give up.

God will give you the abilities you need, too. You may not know you have them at first, but once you start trying to do what God is calling you to do you'll start seeing them, and they'll keep getting better the more you use and develop them.

God will also furnish people to support you, although they may not give you the support you'd like to have. Because they're human, they won't do everything that God wants them to do. And because you're human, you'll probably want some kinds of help that God knows aren't really helpful.

As you respond to God's call and do the ministry that God wants you to do in the world, you'll need to stay in contact with the gathered church, because that is where you're most likely to find the other people who have recognized God's call and chosen to respond to it. They're the ones most likely to give you the support you need, and they need your support for the ministries they're working at.

You may have a hard time finding these people, but they exist, and they need you just as much as you need them. You're both human, remember, so they may not search for you as actively as you'd like. They may even rebuff your efforts to find them, but you can't afford to let that stop you. If you show your interest and keep searching, you'll find the right people. They may not be where you expect to find them, and they may not look like you expect them to look, but they're out there. If you ask God to direct you to them and if you keep your heart and mind open so you can recognize them, you'll find them.

Don't wait for the perfect time, because it won't ever come. You don't have to know any more or understand any better or get your life in better order before coming to God. Jesus made that clear in a story he told. He compared God to a loving father whose son left home in order to live the way he wanted to. When the son finally realized that his way wasn't working he headed back home, but as you can imagine, he was not sure his father would take him back. To his delight he found that not only was his father willing to take him back, but his father didn't even wait for him to get all the way home before coming out to welcome him. "While he was still far off," Jesus said, "his father saw him and was filled with compassion; he ran and put his arms around him and kissed him" (Luke 15:20, NRSV).

God is equally glad to see you coming. You don't have to get any closer than you are right now. As soon as you let God know you're on the way, God will hurry out to meet you.

Even if you're already active in a church and trying to follow God's call, you still need to keep returning to God and searching for the people who can support you in your ministry, whether you're clergy or laity. You also need to be on the lookout for the people who are searching for you—the people God wants you to support. Some of them won't know exactly what they're looking for, and many will be afraid to let you know that they're looking, so they may be hard to recognize.

Some of the searching people may bring prophetic messages that God wants your church to hear. You may not want to hear them, because they will call for change. They will advocate doing things in new ways that may not look desirable or even possible to you. Remember, God's prophetic messengers are nonconformists, rebels, and critics of the status quo. They rock the boat. They make you uncomfortable, because they ask embarrassing questions and point out things you'd rather not see. They question the way you've always done things and the beliefs you've never dared to question. Prophets attack the things that you think are sacred but God knows are idols.

For the church to carry out its God-given ministry, you'll have to do your part, whether you're clergy or laity and whether you're inside the church or outside of it right now. The most effective church congregations are those in which clergy and laity are working together toward a God-given vision. In such congregations the clergy lead and support the laity, but they don't keep too tight a rein on what laypeople do. Laypeople challenge clergy to lead in the way God calls them to lead, not just in the way that the congregation expects. Laypeople support each other, and they take initiative and responsibility for what they see God calling the church to do. They're not passive spectators.

In these congregations outsiders are welcomed, not just tolerated. Church members go out into the world to seek the people God calls them to minister to, and to be God's agents of healing. And the church listens to the prophetic voices within it as well as those who speak from the outside.

Will you risk being part of such a church? If you will, God will give you all the help you need, and the blanks God has left for you to fill will no longer be blank. As one of God's partners you will be helping to put God's plan for the world into effect.

Questions for Reflection

1. What blank do you think God has left for you to fill? How might you go about trying to fill it, with God's help?

2. Where have you looked for people to support you in your efforts to respond to God's call? To what extent have you succeeded in finding them? Have you been surprised by any of the people you found, or by the setting in which you found them? How might you expand your search or change its direction to make it more fruitful?

3. Have searchers ever come to you for support? Did you have any trouble recognizing them as searchers? How did you feel about your ability to furnish what they were looking for? How did you respond?

4. If you are active in a church, what prophetic voices do you think might be bringing a message from God to your church? How are you responding to them? How could you help your church heed what they are saying?

5. If you are not active in a church now, how might you locate a congregation that could help you respond to God's call?

6. Now that you have finished this book, what other thoughts or feelings do you have about the subjects it has addressed? What new insights have you received? What will you consider doing about them?*

Bibliography

Barth, Karl. *Church Dogmatics.* Vols. 3/1 and 4/2. Edinburgh: T. & T. Clark, 1958-1960.

—— *Dogmatics in Outline.* New York: Harper and Brothers, 1959.

Bornkamm, Günther. *Jesus of Nazareth.* New York: Harper and Brothers, 1960.

Brunner, Emil. *The Divine Imperative.* Philadelphia: Westminster Press, 1957.

—— *Man in Revolt.* Philadelphia: Westminster Press, 1957.

Calvin, John. *Institutes.* Vol. 3, part 7. Philadelphia: Westminster Press, 1960.

Carmody, Denise Lardner. *Seizing the Apple: A Feminist Spirituality of Personal Growth.* New York: Crossroad, 1984.

Congar, Yves. *Lay People in the Church.* Westminster, Md.: The Newman Press, 1965.

Fiorenza, Elisabeth Schüssler. *In Memory of Her.* New York: Crossroad, 1985.

Ivins, Molly. *Molly Ivins Can't Say That, Can She?* New York: Random House, 1991.

Kelly, Thomas R. *A Testament of Devotion.* New York: Harper and Row, 1941.

Küng, Hans. *The Church.* New York: Sheed and Ward, 1968.

—— *On Being a Christian.* Garden City, N.Y.: Doubleday and Company, 1976.

Lochman, Jan. *The Faith We Confess.* Philadelphia: Fortress Press, 1984.

Luther, Martin. "The Freedom of a Christian." *Luther's Works,* vol. 31. Philadelphia: Muhlenberg Press, 1958.

Michalson, Carl. *Faith for Personal Crises.* New York: Charles Scribner's Sons, 1958.

—— *The Hinge of History.* New York: Charles Scribner's Sons, 1959.

Maas, Peter. *Marie.* New York: Pocket Books, 1983.

Moltmann, Jürgen. *The Crucified God.* New York: Harper and Row, 1974.

—— *The Trinity and the Kingdom.* New York: Harper and Row, 1981.

Niebuhr, Reinhold. *The Nature and Destiny of Man.* Vol. 1. New York: Charles Scribner's Sons, 1953.

Norris, Richard A. *Understanding the Faith of the Church.* New York: The Seabury Press, 1979.

Ruether, Rosemary Radford. *The Radical Kingdom.* New York: Paulist Press, 1970.

Shaffer, Peter. *Amadeus.* New York: Harper and Row, 1980.

Tillich, Paul. *Systematic Theology.* Vols. 1 and 2. Chicago: The University of Chicago Press, 1951-1959.

Wilson, Patricia. *How Can I Be Over the Hill When I Haven't Seen the Top Yet?: Faithful Reflections on the Middle Years of Life.* Nashville: Upper Room Books, 1989.